Julie H. Ferguson

Julie H. Ferguson is the author of *Sing a New Song: Portraits of Canada's Crusading Bishops* (2006), *Through a Canadian Periscope: The Story of the Canadian Submarine Service* (1995), and eleven other books, including five for writers and teachers.

Not only is Julie a successful author, she is also an accomplished speaker and trainer. Since 1997, many of western Canada's school districts have invited her back time and again to present at their professional development events and to lead lively writing workshops for their gifted, regular, and special education students. Julie delights in inspiring participants in boys-only English classes and aboriginal students to improve their writing. Currently, she lives in Port Moody, B near Vancouver. Visit her at *www.beaconlit.com*.

In the Same Collection

Ven Begamudré, *Isaac Brock: Larger Than Life*
Lynne Bowen, *Robert Dunsmuir: Laird of the Mines*
Kate Braid, *Emily Carr: Rebel Artist*
Kathryn Bridge, *Phyllis Munday: Mountaineer*
William Chalmers, *George Mercer Dawson: Geologist, Scientist, Explorer*
Anne Cimon, *Susanna Moodie: Pioneer Author*
Deborah Cowley, *Lucille Teasdale: Doctor of Courage*
Gary Evans, *John Grierson: Trailblazer of Documentary Film*
Judith Fitzgerald, *Marshall McLuhan: Wise Guy*
lian goodall, *William Lyon Mackenzie King: Dreams and Shadows*
Tom Henighan, *Vilhjalmur Stefansson: Arctic Adventurer*
Stephen Eaton Hume, *Frederick Banting: Hero, Healer, Artist*
Naïm Kattan, *A.M. Klein: Poet and Prophet*
Betty Keller, *Pauline Johnson: First Aboriginal Voice of Canada*
Heather Kirk, *Mazo de la Roche: Rich and Famous Writer*
Vladimir Konieczny, *Glenn Gould: A Musical Force*
Michelle Labrèche-Larouche, *Emma Albani: International Star*
Wayne Larsen, *A.Y. Jackson: A Love for the Land*
Wayne Larsen, *James Wilson Morrice: Painter of Light and Shadow*
Francine Legaré, *Samuel de Champlain: Father of New France*
Margaret Macpherson, *Nellie McClung: Voice for the Voiceless*
Nicholas Maes, *Robertson Davies: Magician of Words*
Dave Margoshes, *Tommy Douglas: Building the New Society*
Marguerite Paulin, *René Lévesque: Charismatic Leader*
Marguerite Paulin, *Maurice Duplessis: Powerbroker, Politician*
Raymond Plante, *Jacques Plante: Behind the Mask*
Jim Poling Sr., *Tecumseh: Shooting Star, Crouching Panther*
T.F. Rigelhof, *George Grant: Redefining Canada*
Tom Shardlow, *David Thompson: A Trail by Stars*
Arthur Slade, *John Diefenbaker: An Appointment with Destiny*
Roderick Stewart, *Wilfrid Laurier: A Pledge for Canada*
Sharon Stewart, *Louis Riel: Firebrand*
André Vanasse, *Gabrielle Roy: A Passion for Writing*
John Wilson, *John Franklin: Traveller on Undiscovered Seas*
John Wilson, *Norman Bethune: A Life of Passionate Conviction*
Rachel Wyatt, *Agnes Macphail: Champion of the Underdog*

DOUGLAS

James

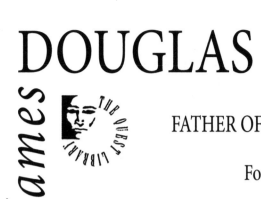

FATHER OF BRITISH COLUMBIA

Foreword by Stephen Hume

DUNDURN PRESS
TORONTO

Editor: Michael Carroll
Index: Julie H. Ferguson
Design: Courtney Horner
Printer: Webcom

Library and Archives Canada Cataloguing in Publication

Ferguson, Julie H., 1945-
    James Douglas : father of British Columbia / by Julie H. Ferguson.

Includes bibliographical references and index.
ISBN 978-1-55488-409-4

    1. Douglas, James, Sir, 1803-1877. 2. British
Columbia--History--1849-1871. 3. Northwest, Canadian--History--To 1870.
4. Governors--British Columbia--Biography. 5. Fur traders--Canada,
Western--Biography. I. Title.

FC3822.1.D68 F47 2009   971.1'02092   C2009-900494-1

1   2   3   4   5   13   12   11   10   09

  Conseil des Arts   Canada Council    ONTARIO ARTS COUNCIL
du Canada   for the Arts   CONSEIL DES ARTS DE L'ONTARIO

We acknowledge the support of the **Canada Council for the Arts** and the **Ontario Arts Council** for our publishing program. We also acknowledge the financial support of the **Government of Canada** through the **Book Publishing Industry Development Program** and **The Association for the Export of Canadian Books**, and the **Government of Ontario** through the **Ontario Book Publishers Tax Credit program**, and the **Ontario Media Development Corporation**.

Printed and bound in Canada.
Printed on recycled paper.

www.dundurn.com

Mixed Sources
Product group from well-managed
forests, and other controlled sources
www.fsc.org Cert no. SW-COC-002358
© 1996 Forest Stewardship Council
FSC

Dundurn Press   Gazelle Book Services Limited   Dundurn Press
3 Church Street, Suite 500   White Cross Mills   2250 Military Road
Toronto, Ontario, Canada   High Town, Lancaster, England   Tonawanda, NY
M5E 1M2   LA1 4XS   U.S.A. 14150

Contents

Foreword

The teenager leaning on the rail as big grey Atlantic swells hissed under the heeling sides of the square-rigged sailing ship *Matthews* was fifteen. He was fresh out of school and leaving Scotland on a bold adventure that would take him to the edge of the known world.

In time James Douglas would be called "Old Square-Toes" and would gain a reputation for being a bit stuffy and strict. But that was later, after he grew up and earned the right to put "Sir" in front of his name for services to Queen Victoria in creating British Columbia and keeping Canada's Pacific province from falling into American hands.

Back in 1819, though, he was a curious, adventurous lad looking forward to his new job and a chance to make his fortune in North America. Behind him, Europe recovered from the Napoleonic Wars, really the first genuine "world war." It had even drawn in the two new countries of Canada and the United States. Only five years before James sailed across the Atlantic, Americans had attacked Canada and the British had burned the White House. There was an uneasy, watchful peace, but in the Far West, where the teenager was bound, borders were uncertain, there were few maps, and people in Europe knew less about it than we know about Mars.

So James, who celebrated his sixteenth birthday at sea, really was sailing into a new world at an age when teenagers today are taking driving lessons and worrying about whether they'll be grounded for coming home too late from the movies. Before James was eighteen he fought his first duel and climbed into a birchbark canoe with a skin scarcely thicker than a pizza box to travel wild rivers into the unmapped heart of a vast continent. There he met and mingled with warrior chiefs wearing beaded buckskin and feather headdresses, explorers who had been where no European had gone before, the French-Canadian *coureurs de bois* who slipped through dark, frozen forests like ghosts, Scots fur traders who played their bagpipes when they came into camp, and dashing Métis buffalo hunters.

He married the pretty granddaughter of a Cree chief, helped end one of Canada's few real wars between First Nations and settlers, and brought law and order to the unruly gold rush boom camps and an elected government to the huge colonial territory he came to govern.

Julie Ferguson tells the astonishing story of this teenager who came to be known as the Father of British Columbia and whose work shaped the continent, the countries, the states, and the provinces we all share and call North America today.

Stephen Hume

Journalist and Author of *Simon Fraser: In Search of Modern British Columbia*

Author's Note

Most excerpts from James Douglas's letters and journal scattered throughout this book are fictional representations of real documents. Others rely on the imagination of the author where no archival material exists. However, all are based on historical facts and events, as well as what is known of Douglas's character.

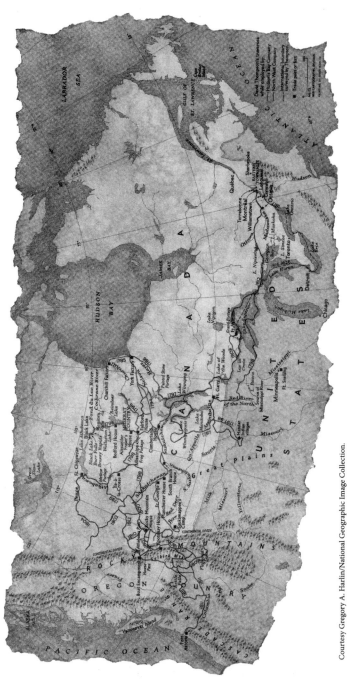

A modern version of the David Thompson map of the North West Company's empire, 1814, that hung in the Great Hall at Fort William (Thunder Bay, Ontario, today).

1

Contrasts and Comparisons

Today Canadians travel from Vancouver to Montreal in five and a half hours by air. Roads criss-cross the country, linking towns big and small, regions urban and rural. A train gets a traveller east to west in a few days. Cars are a necessity for families rather than a luxury. So are maps. James Douglas thought nothing of journeying five thousand kilometres with none of that.

Our homes and workplaces keep us warm in winter and cool in summer. We have light at the touch of a switch. We telephone or text friends anywhere in the world. We access the latest weather forecasts and communicate instantly on the Internet. James Douglas operated with none of that.

In 2008, the 150th anniversary of British Columbia, I sat in my condominium in Metro Vancouver and pondered how the founder of the province did it. The more I thought the more

I came to understand what a feat it was to survive in Canada between 1819 and 1877, let alone stickhandle two gold rushes and lead two colonies on the outer fringes of the civilized world.

I wondered, too, how James Douglas lived and travelled. How did he cope with no toilet paper, no Kleenex, no shampoo, no hot water? What happened if he got sick or injured? How did he manage winter travel with only Hudson's Bay blankets and no sleeping bag, the summers with mosquitoes and no bug repellent? How did he journey thousands of kilometres through the wilderness, over the Rocky Mountains seven times, with only the power of his own arms and legs?

James Douglas thrived on hardship. In 1812, at the age of nine, he was plucked from his mother and sent to live with strangers while he went to school for six years. At fifteen he sailed alone across the Atlantic Ocean to apprentice with a fur-trading company based in Montreal. A few days later he canoed with *voyageurs* through 1,230 kilometres of wilderness to Fort William (Thunder Bay) to begin his career.

By the time Douglas chose the location of present-day Victoria, British Columbia, in the mid-1800s, he had already lived on the frontier of the New World for twenty-three years, often in primitive conditions. He had experienced a rugged, untamed land that took months to cross on foot or horseback, by canoe or sled. But where many failed he flourished. Douglas rose steadily from lowly clerk to fur trader, and on up to manage a fort and later a region. He spent much of this time in the huge Columbia Department of the Hudson's Bay Company that lay west of the Rockies and stretched from Russian Alaska to the Columbia River in today's Oregon.

When Douglas first stepped onto southern Vancouver Island, he was thirty-nine years old and had a part-Cree wife and three children. He guided Victoria's development into a successful settlement. When Vancouver Island became a Crown Colony, he became its second governor. A few years later a huge gold rush to the Fraser River propelled the British government to declare the mainland a colony, too. Queen Victoria named it British Columbia and, again, Douglas as its governor. Just before he retired in 1864, she knighted him in recognition for his services to the empire.

James Douglas's achievements were extraordinary and intricately woven through the heart of Canadian and Pacific Northwest history when it was a wild land and British Columbia didn't exist. Given his obscure origins and early experiences, Douglas's triumph was even more spectacular. In some ways he was a most unlikely "Father of British Columbia" and, in others, ideal. This is his story. And ours.

2

Beginnings and Endings

In 2008 a statue was unveiled in South America, and British Columbia celebrated its 150th birthday. What was the connection? A curious one, to be sure.

The larger-than-life bronze statue that commemorates Sir James Douglas, the first governor of British Columbia, stands on waste ground in front of an unremarkable single-storey building in Mahaica, a village in Guyana, formerly British Guiana. The statue looks oddly out of place in this tropical village with its waving palm trees. The man it represents wears a buttoned vest, long trousers, a tight cravat around his neck, and a thick coat with the collar turned up as if warding off a chilly wind. Imposing, certainly, but strange.

The South American statue is identical to the one that graces Fort Langley on the Fraser River in British Columbia. Indeed, the Guyanese government had the statue cast from the

The two identical statues of James Douglas: left in Guyana; right at Fort Langley, British Columbia.

original mould in British Columbia so they could honour their native son of whom they are so proud. The Guyanese believe James Douglas's life is inspirational — proof that individuals can achieve greatness from modest beginnings.

The story starts with Douglas's mother, Martha Ann Ritchie. Her family was originally from Barbados, and she was the daughter of a white man and a black mother who was neither poor nor a slave. In British Guiana, women of mixed race like Martha Ann were known as free coloured, but how much black blood ran in James's mother's veins is a mystery. It may have been half-and-half, a quarter, or even an eighth. Both Martha Ann and her mother, Rebecca, could read and write and were businesswomen of some standing in their Guianese community in the early 1800s.

James's father was John, Scottish and white. He came from a wealthy Glasgow family that had extensive trade interests in the British colonies of the West Indies of which British Guiana was considered a part. When learning the business, John spent years at a time overseeing his family's sugar plantations there, only occasionally returning to Scotland. During his time in Guiana, John was involved in a long and intimate liaison with Martha Ann.

John and Martha Ann's relationship resulted in two children — Alexander in 1801 and James in 1803 — but there was no expectation of marriage on either side. The boys took their father's last name and lived quietly with their mother and grandmother while their father attended to his plantations and company business when he wasn't in Scotland.

On a trip back to Glasgow in 1809, James's father, now forty-one, married Jessie Hamilton, the young daughter of another prominent merchant family. The couple set up a sizable home together, anticipating a large family. Following the death of his father in 1810, John decided he would live permanently in Scotland. So, in mid-1811, he paid a year-long visit to Guiana without his Scottish wife to deal with business and break the news to Martha Ann that he wouldn't be back. Nevertheless, he didn't abandon his "first" family completely.

John found his young sons dark-skinned from the sun and their heritage, healthy, and speaking with a Guianese accent. Lightly dressed, barefoot much of the time, and running free, the brothers enjoyed playing in the endless sunshine. Thanks to the secure, stable environment their grandmother and mother provided for the growing boys, they had a happy early childhood. On arrival John rekindled his affair with Martha Ann Ritchie, and she conceived their third child. In 1812 she gave birth to Cecilia, whom John named after his Scottish grandmother and sister.

James Douglas was illegitimate, born outside marriage, and partly black. Polite society considered illegitimate offspring unacceptable, though they were a common result of men spending many years in the colonies without their wives. James's father wasn't ashamed of his three natural children, but he was acutely aware his relatives might be offended if he brought them openly into the family in Glasgow. John also knew his Guianese boys would have to make their own way in the world — only his legitimate sons would inherit his property and wealth. Before he sailed from Scotland, John made plans for his sons to receive the best education he could afford to improve their chances of success. Up until then Alexander and James had attended a local school that taught only the barest essentials. It was an inadequate education for what their father had in mind for them.

After Cecilia was born, John announced he had enrolled James and Alexander in a good Scottish school. How Martha Ann reacted to this can only be imagined. James was just nine years old when he kissed his mother goodbye. He never saw her again.

3

A Life Change

James Douglas stood on a wooden crate to see over the ship's rail. Alone he stood vigil, never taking his eyes off the land of his birth until it vanished. When his father joined him, James asked him when they would return and see his mother.

"Not for a very long time. You have at least six years at school in Scotland first."

James bit his lower lip to stop it from quivering. He didn't want to be a weakling, but it was hard not to cry. "What is Glasgow like, Papa?" he managed to ask.

"Very different. It has grey skies much of the time. It's cold in winter and there's snow. The city is big with lots of brick houses and many people. Carriages and carts fill the roads. There are factories, smoke, and soot."

A solitary tear escaped and ran down James's cheek. "It ... it doesn't sound very nice."

The youngster felt his father's hand on his shoulder. "You'll get used to it — men do, you know. And don't forget. You'll see me often."

James wondered what that meant. Surely, he'd see him every day.

"Could you find Alexander, please?" James's father asked as he turned to go below. "I want to talk to you in my cabin before dinner. I have something important to say to you both."

James felt his anticipation of the six-week voyage to the Old World bleed away. The pain of parting from his mother, coupled with his father's words, unsettled him. James was also uncomfortable. His new, unfamiliar clothes made him hot and restricted his movement. He longed for the loose shirts and short trousers he had always worn that his father had made him leave behind. The only things James did like were the sensation of the ship rising and falling to the ocean swell and the creak of the rigging now that they were far out to sea.

He sought out his brother, who was playing listlessly with the ship's cat in the shade on the leeward side of the deck. James told him they had to go to their father's cabin.

"Don't want to," Alexander said.

"We must. Papa said so. Come on!" James noticed his brother's pale lips and the sweat on his brow.

"I'll follow you in a minute."

James reluctantly went below to join his father, certain there was more bad news to come.

"I called you to my cabin to tell you something important. Something I couldn't tell you before we left." James's father licked his lips. "In Scotland I have another family. I married three years ago, and my wife's name is Jessie."

James held his breath until he thought he would burst.

"Jessie and I hope to have a large family. We live in a big house in Glasgow."

"So there's lots of room for us?" James ventured.

"Not exactly." His father stood and leaned against the closed door. "You see, because your mother and I weren't married, you can't live with my wife and me. It's not acceptable in Scotland to have one's natural children mothered by one's own wife."

James had no idea what his father was talking about, but dared not ask him to explain.

"You'll be going to a very good school in Lanark outside Glasgow and living with a family called Glendenning. I'll visit you as often as I can."

"Can we visit you?" James asked.

"Not at my home." His father crossed the cabin and peered out of the porthole.

"So we're outcasts," Alexander said. He rushed out and slammed the door.

Young James bit his lip again and blinked. His father sat on the stool beside him and offered his handkerchief. This time James couldn't stop his tears. His father waited until he cried himself out, then said, "I have to see to Alex. I think he's seasick, poor chap."

James sat patiently while his father put Alexander to bed, a bucket by his side and a cool, wet cloth on his forehead. James thought of the questions he needed answered. As they waited for dinnertime, his father told him a lot more about his "other" family who, James discovered, did know of their existence. James learned what "illegitimate" meant, as well as "mixed race." He heard that his white blood came from a large, intermarrying, business elite of considerable wealth and influence. James listened intently so he could tell Alexander everything when his brother felt better. Then his father changed the subject.

"I know, Jamie, how difficult this move is for you, as well as what I've just told you. It's normal to be upset and confused about it all. Ask me all the questions you want. You'll survive, I promise." His father ruffled James's curly hair.

"You see, it's all about how one chooses to deal with the bad stuff. I'll teach you how to do it while we're at sea." James nodded uncertainly. "I'll teach you how to deal with boredom, too — a very important skill for men. We'll do lessons together every morning so I can tell your new school how much you've both learned so far, and we'll take exercise every afternoon to keep healthy." As soon as his father finished speaking, James followed him into dinner, leaving Alexander to sleep.

The boys quickly discovered that life onboard ship wasn't as exciting as they had expected. They were stuck in a very small world that didn't provide much fun after the initial novelty wore off. But their father kept his word and made sure they were busy. Every morning, except on Sundays, he led their lessons. He gave them fat notebooks to use as journals and insisted they write in them daily. He taught them to observe the natural world and draw what they saw. He drilled them in arithmetic and helped them read aloud from the books he had brought for them. He borrowed the captain's globe and taught them geography, which James took to immediately.

Over the next while James made several attempts to tell his brother what he had learned about the family from his father, but Alexander didn't seem interested. The older Douglas boy spent most of his spare time whittling sticks as the sailors did. Soon James stopped asking Alexander to play with him and got on with what he wanted to do.

James's father helped him ease the separation from his mother. "She's missing you a great deal, too, you know," he said a couple of days into the voyage. "She would enjoy getting letters from you. You could easily write a kind of diary letter."

"What's that?" James asked.

"Well, a couple of times a week tell Mama what you've done, what you've seen, what you've learned. Put the date above each entry. Then I can add your pages to the letter I'll send her from each port we visit. You should continue to write to her when you're at school, too."

James thought for a moment. "I can even copy some of what I write in my notebook, can't I?"

"Yes. Mama will write back to you, as well. That way you can keep in touch."

James loved his lesson time with his father. He asked questions endlessly and made rapid progress. His father kept the promise to show both boys how to amuse themselves in the hours outside lesson time. James was soon devouring books so fast that he ran out and had to borrow more from the other passengers and the captain. Alexander was unenthusiastic about everything.

While onboard, James developed his ability to focus for long stretches and how to find out about items he was interested in. He jotted down notes about things that caught his fancy — dolphins, the weather, how ships sail, and the stars, for example. He asked the first mate to show him the constellations and even tried his hand at learning to navigate using a sextant. He looked up dolphins in one of the captain's books and pestered him about the weather. The captain, a father himself, kindly showed James a little about how to forecast by studying the waves and the sky.

One day James persuaded a sailor to help him climb the rigging to the crow's nest. His father quickly put a stop to that and encouraged the boys to play tag on deck instead. On Sunday mornings the three attended Divine Service on the poop deck led by the captain, after which their father read passages from the Bible to them. He explained the meaning behind the verses he had chosen, and James began to learn the Christian values of compassion and responsibility for others. His father encouraged the boys to discuss philosophical topics with him and guided them in solving problems by thinking through situations he put forward.

By the time the ship approached Liverpool, James realized he had changed. He was quite different from the boy who had climbed the gangplank six weeks earlier. He was more self-reliant and could occupy himself quite contentedly when necessary. He was also aware his father was proud of him. However, James was saddened by Alexander's withdrawal — they had lost the closeness they had enjoyed in Guiana, but he didn't understand why. He did see that his brother hadn't enjoyed his lessons, couldn't settle to a book, and didn't deal with boredom well.

The night before they arrived in Liverpool, James and Alexander listened as their father outlined the plans for their first few days ashore.

"Tomorrow we'll set out for Glasgow and stay in a hotel there one night. Then I'll take you to Mrs. Glendenning's in Lanark where you'll live while you go to school."

"When do we start school?" James asked.

"September 15. But we'll visit the school before I return to Glasgow, so you can look around and meet the headmaster and teachers."

"Must we wear uniforms?" Alexander asked.

"Oh, yes, I'll kit you out properly. After that all you have to do is ask Mrs. Glendenning for things you need, and I'll pay her for what she buys you. Ponies not included!"

4

Scotland and School

In Scotland, James Douglas continued his journal and also wrote letters, though not as regularly as he had, for schoolwork quickly intervened. Neither his notebooks nor his letters from his youth survive, so James's first impressions of Glasgow and his new life, and the reactions of others to his arrival, are lost. However, several things are certain: the move to Scotland was a wrench, the culture shock extreme, and the climate miserable in comparison to Guiana.

Whether his extended family provided any welcome or extended any invitations to the boys is unknown but unlikely. James was certainly curious about his relatives, but had to be content with the details his father chose to give. James met none of his kin until half a century later when he achieved considerable standing in his own right and his grandparents, father, and stepmother had passed away.

John Douglas delivered James and Alexander to Mrs. Glendenning and settled them in. Her house was high on a hill above the River Clyde and the vast cotton mills of New Lanark, thirty-five kilometres southeast of Glasgow. James immediately felt comfortable in the ordinary home near the school they were to attend, but he was less sure of the school. Lanark Grammar School, built of pinkish-brown stone typical of the region, was quite unlike his easygoing one-room school in Guiana. His immediate impression on looking around was one of size and austerity.

"It'll feel better when it's filled with pupils," his father remarked when he saw James's crestfallen face. "I expect you thought all schools look the same. Let's go and meet the headmaster."

James and Alexander trailed inside after their father. Their new headmaster looked strict and wore a black sleeveless coat over his tweed suit. James was surprised that he didn't talk to him or his brother, but only to his father. He wondered why they had had to come if the headmaster wasn't interested in getting to know his new students.

A couple of days later, after the frenzy of buying uniforms and books, John Douglas departed for Glasgow and his wife. Standing at the door of the boys' new home, he told them, "I want you to study hard, always behave properly, and obey Mrs. Glendenning and your teachers at all times. I'll visit you in the middle of October." Then he kissed James and Alexander farewell. They were on their own.

John Douglas had chosen Lanark Grammar School for his boys because of its reputation for turning out well-educated students. The 650-year-old fee-paying school delivered a classical curriculum emphasizing Latin and Greek, which also included French, mathematics, geography, and bookkeeping.[1] On September 15, 1812, the two boys joined their ninety fellow pupils to begin a rigorous education to prepare them for what their father hoped would be successful lives. James, preoccupied with all the changes in his life, had no clue that his father had already mapped out a career for him that would take him as far away from his Scottish family as possible.

November 7, 1812

> Dear Papa,
> I am greatly in need of an atlas of the world. Mrs. Glendenning says that I can't get one in Lanark, so I am hoping you can find one for me. Please bring it the next time you come. I am well and hope you are, too.
>
> Your affectionate son,
> James

James's father had difficulty finding an atlas, for they were rare in the early 1800s. When he did, he decided with typical Scottish stinginess that it was far too expensive an item for a young boy. James, disappointed, had to settle for a globe instead.

Soon James adjusted to his situation and began to enjoy his lessons. His father had topped up most of his missing knowledge on the ship, but he had to start from scratch with Latin and Greek. Friends were more difficult to come by. The other students already had friends and didn't include the Douglas boys in their tight circles. James felt his differences acutely. Among Scots boys with pale complexions, his black hair and dark skin stood out and were noticed. Classmates mocked his strange accent, too, and James had difficulty deciphering their thick Glaswegian dialect.

December 15, 1812

Dear Mr. Douglas,

As requested, here is the report on your sons' first term with us.

Your elder son, Alexander, is not progressing as well as he should. He is lazy and his mind does not move quickly enough to learn at the pace of his class. He lacks intelligence. However, as he continues to adjust, his masters are hopeful he will improve.

James, on the other hand, is doing better than we expected. He is intelligent, inquiring, and hard-working. His favourite subjects are geography and accounting; he is progressing with Latin and Greek. James enjoys sports and is developing physically as he should. We anticipate he will do very well in our school.

Your obedient servant,
Headmaster,
Lanark Grammar School

James made great strides in French, not just the French of classrooms and exercise books but real conversational French. He had a natural ear for languages, which his father encouraged by engaging a tutor for him, knowing full well he would need the tongue in the future. James's teacher was a French prisoner of war captured during the Napoleonic Wars, and the pair met regularly for several years. By the time James left Lanark, he was fluent — able to speak, read, and write excellent French.

Throughout his school days James made time for his fascination with nature. He roamed the hillsides and riverbanks around Lanark, often with his landlady's daughter, who was a couple of years his senior. She became his best friend and filled the gap created by Alexander's withdrawal. Once James had stopped yearning for the tropics, he grew to love the fertile beauty of the Clyde Valley. When he needed to think things through or if he was lonely, he drew solace from frequent, long tramps in any weather through the lush, green countryside. The habit stuck.

James occasionally had difficult times at school, not with academics but probably with taunts of classmates. In letters he wrote later in life, he admitted fighting his way out of several situations due to his tendency to lose his temper when provoked. He lost his Guianese accent as fast as he could and never mentioned his two families. By the time he left school, he had learned to conceal his origins completely.

April 3, 1819

Dear Mama,

I have nearly finished school here in Scotland. You will be pleased to hear that I got high marks in all subjects and now my French, thanks to Papa, is excellent. I'm going to need it.

It seems a lifetime since I was with you and Grandmamma. You would not recognize me I'm so tall! I'm sorry to let you know that I will not be able to visit you before I start my new job in the fur trade that Papa has arranged for me. Perhaps later.

I pray that you are well and happy. How is Cecilia?

Until next time, your affectionate son,
James

Few other clues exist to help us imagine James's life in Lanark. He did keep in touch with his mother, but did he correspond regularly with his father, too? How often did he see his father? Did he see his other Scottish relatives during the school holidays? There are some hints that James may have occasionally visited Orbiston House, his Aunt Cecilia's estate that lay on the road from Lanark to Glasgow. Most probably, though, the boys spent their vacations with the Glendennings in Lanark.

In their early years it was Mrs. Glendenning who comforted the boys when they were homesick and lonely, dried their tears, nursed them when they were ill, and celebrated their successes. James grew to care deeply for his surrogate mother, and when she fell on hard times as she aged, he sent money to her.

From the perspective of nearly two centuries later, it may seem cruel to uproot a small boy of nine from his mother and all that he had known and loved to send him thousands of kilometres across the Atlantic to live with strangers. However, it was a common practice in colonial times. Many boys attending boarding schools didn't have the benefit of living with a family as the Douglas boys did and didn't see their parents for years, often as much as a decade. Fortunately, James Douglas had a more comfortable and happier upbringing in Lanark while he acquired an education and saw his father regularly. Even so, the experience strengthened James, and he learned to rely on himself as his father had promised. James developed a confidence during his school days that escaped his brother.

Once he reached adulthood, James pulled a veil over his origins and early life. For many years he remained secretive about his childhood with his most intimate family, too, and wrote about it even less. In a culture that was more intolerant than today, he learned at a young age he must hide the shame of his illegitimacy and his black blood if he was to succeed. He began to measure his achievements by the only standard he knew — the white standard within a white-dominated world. He never considered his successes from the perspective of a part-black man. Even after he received his knighthood and reconnected with his Scottish family, Douglas still wrestled with these two stigmas. Perhaps, like many black and mixed blood men today, his birth circumstances and race were at the root of an internal drive that made him prove his worth all his life.

5

A Nor'wester in the Fur Trade

James Douglas turned at the top of the gangplank for a final wave to his father who stood below him on the dock at Liverpool. They had bid farewell to each other privately in tight control of their emotions and now faced the moment of parting. The teenage Douglas readjusted the duffle on his shoulder that contained his precious books and notebooks and headed for his cabin without a backward glance. His father climbed into the carriage for the journey back to Glasgow. Neither could bear to prolong the moment; both hoped they would see each other again, but knew they might not.

John Douglas had not only educated his sons but had also arranged careers for them. He sent both off to British North America (Canada) to join the North West Company (NWC) where they were to work for six years as indentured apprentices in the fur trade. John could have employed his sons in the family business in the colonies, but he chose not to, perhaps because the plantations weren't doing well or possibly because he didn't want his sons returning to Glasgow anytime soon. So the Douglas boys followed in the footsteps of many Scottish lads who went to work for NWC rather than the more English Hudson's Bay Company (HBC). Alexander had made the journey in 1818 when he was seventeen and James, a year later, at fifteen.

By the time James left British shores, he had done his homework on the fur trade. He knew that a Royal Charter of 1670 from King Charles II of England had established HBC more than a century before NWC. The charter granted HBC all the land in the vast Hudson Bay watershed and a monopoly on the Native fur trade within it. Beaver, otter, marten, and other animal pelts brought high profits in a European market greedy for furs. However, by the time James arrived, the animals were already decreasing due to over-trapping. From their North American headquarters at York Factory on Hudson Bay, HBC controlled more land than any other company in the world and acted like a government, even issuing its own money at one point. But it was the directors in England who made the decisions.

James knew that, by contrast, merchant investors of Scottish heritage led the North West Company from Montreal. This company had developed out of growing resentment to HBC's monopoly and operated farther west where the fur-bearing animals were still plentiful. NWC's collection centre for furs was at Fort William on Lake Superior. NWC's operations expanded ever westward in search of better harvests, and it was from the Lake Athabasca region in the far northwest that the secondary, but no less important, company activity radiated. This was the exploration of routes through the Rockies to the Pacific Ocean.

James's heroes soon became great explorers such as David Thompson and Simon Fraser.

In early May 1819, James Douglas strode onboard the brig *Matthews*, eager for his next adventure to begin. He was bound for Quebec City, arriving just as the furs from the previous year's harvest began to pour into NWC's depots. He knew where Montreal was — his old globe had shown him that — but his father's treasured gift of a map of North America made him wonder what the rest of the country was like. The map showed the land west of the Great Lakes devoid of features except the Rockies, a few lakes, and some rivers, and gave a sense of the enormous distances. After James dumped his bag on his bunk, his father's advice from seven years before echoed through his mind: "Work hard, behave properly, and obey your teachers!"

Douglas hurried ashore six weeks after setting sail to catch a river steamer to Montreal. Here he handed his body and soul over to the North West Company. His indenture would rule his every thought and action for six years. Apprentices earned a total income for the six years of £100, none of which Douglas would receive until the end of his contract. In the meantime the company undertook to feed, house, equip, and train him.

Montreal, July 7, 1819

Dear Papa,

This is a hasty note, penned so it will catch a ship before I disappear into the wilderness. I wanted to reassure you I arrived in Montreal safely and signed my papers at the North West Company offices today. The contract clauses reminded me of your instructions when I was nine, and I plan to apply them to guide my life. I also promised to keep NWC secrets and never embezzle, waste, or unlawfully dispose of company assets. At last I'm a Nor'wester! I hope to do well and earn your faith in me.

I join a party that leaves from Lachine, a short way west of here, bound for Fort William. I'm told it may take four to six weeks to get there. I hope I survive the journey, for it sounds demanding.

Your loving son,
James

His orders were to join a brigade two days hence in Lachine, the company's huge storage depot beside the St. Lawrence River west of Montreal. He didn't know exactly what a brigade was, but soon discovered it was a convoy of ten canoes. He wondered why canoes were the method of transport instead of horses and carts.

Next morning activity on the wharf seethed around Douglas. He watched men in furs, Natives in fringed and beaded buckskin, and businessmen in fancy waistcoats. His eight travelling companions greeted him with a brisk "B'jour!" and he said "Bonjour!" back in his best French. To Douglas at first glance, the *voyageurs* appeared to be ruffians — swaggering and unruly. They yelled boisterous greetings to one another as they gestured with short pipes filled with tobacco. Each carried a painted paddle over his shoulder and sported a multi-coloured *ceinture fléchée* (sash) to hold up his canvas trousers. On their heads bobbed red or blue woolly caps. In fact, they were *Canadiens* from the farms along the St. Lawrence River, supplemented by a few Natives who made a living transporting the company's furs and supplies back and forth to Fort William, a one-way distance of nearly a thousand kilometres. Douglas learned the crews were *mangeurs de lard* or pork-eaters. One called François handed Douglas his blanket, trousers, shirt, and shoes. He stuffed them into his bag, which was stowed under the huge oilcloth that protected the cargo and provisions in the forward section of the canoe.

When the *voyageurs* waved their caps in the air and the order "Away!" rang out, the crowd on the wharf cried farewell. The paddles dipped deep into the water, and the canoes surged forward at a speed that made the teenager catch his breath. Douglas left civilization for the first time in his life, unaware it would be forty-five years before he returned.

Douglas rode as a passenger in the middle of a huge eleven-metre birchbark *canot de maître* or Montreal canoe, packed to the gunwales with three thousand kilograms of cargo in sixty-four bales. The fully loaded canoe had only a hand span of clearance above the water. The weather was hot and sticky. Thunderstorms drenched Douglas and mosquitoes bit him until he bled. He clung to his seat when the canoe bucked and twisted under him as it tore through white water and sometimes came close to capsizing. He ate a greasy mush of cornmeal laced with fat pork at all meals, sometimes supplemented with fresh or dried berries, and snacked on pemmican to stop his stomach from rumbling. He got dirtier and smellier, a state of affairs he disliked. Occasionally, he passed wooden crosses on riverbanks where travellers had perished, an eloquent warning of ever-present dangers.

At his first portage Douglas blushed scarlet when François hoisted him onto his shoulders to prevent him stepping in the icy water. He vowed never to let *that* happen again, but did when told he had to allow it. Despite his above-average strength and

A huge canot de maître, similar to the one James Douglas rode from Lachine to Fort William in 1819, running rapids on the Ottawa River.

stamina, portaging around rapids was muscle-numbing. Early on the brigade made ten portages in eight kilometres on the Ottawa River, and Douglas nearly dropped from exhaustion. The *voyageurs* often hefted two, even three, bales at a time. Douglas tried lifting one but couldn't carry it very far. Although he didn't have to carry anything as a passenger, he made himself useful by carting paddles and smaller items. Douglas started out counting the portages and reached thirty-six before the brigade arrived at the Great Lakes. But he never once complained.

On the plus side, in calm water he had time to observe the plants and animals of this new world as he glided swiftly along. The huge deciduous trees changed to pines and spruce as he went west, eagles circled overhead, and a couple of moose lumbered out of the bush farther north. Up at dawn, the strong *voyageurs* sang lustily as they paddled, and they taught Douglas the songs and their skills. He was soon paddling at thirty to forty strokes a minute but couldn't sustain the punishing rhythm for sixteen or more hours a day like his companions. The short nights around campfires filled Douglas's ears with stories of other voyages and the fur trade, all in French. He learned to slumber in his clothes on the hard ground wrapped in a blanket, and despite the discomfort, fell asleep instantly, only to awake at dawn after only five or six hours of rest. Always he was too tired to write a single word in his journal.

Douglas marvelled at how fast the brigade moved through a landscape with no roads — their highways were the lakes and rivers of the vast country. They paddled along the St. Lawrence and Ottawa rivers toward Georgian Bay on Lake Huron, then west to Sault Ste. Marie into Lake Superior. This lake, which Douglas knew wasn't a sea, felt like one, with its perils of sudden storms, big waves, and even fog. A lengthy paddle along its north shore got them to Fort William at its western end on August 6. Just before the brigade pulled alongside the great wharf, they stopped at a nearby beach. The *voyageurs* washed, shaved, and donned their best clothes, the ones Douglas had first seen them wearing. He did likewise — at least he made a pretense of shaving — and donned his knee breeches, boots, and knee-length coat again.

With a burst of energy and their favourite *chanson*, the *voyageurs* paddled at full tilt for the fort to a ripple of musket fire called *feu de joie*. Then Douglas heard the frenzied barking of dogs and the shouts of excited residents as they raced to greet the canoes. The *voyageurs* hurriedly unloaded to get to the mess hall for their well-earned meal of extra rations — venison with fresh bread and butter, washed down with a tot of rum.

Douglas was as eager to see his first fort as he was for hot water. As the brigade shipped their paddles, he realized Fort

William was bigger than he had expected and not as primitive as he had feared. The fort stood in a clearing among tall evergreens on the edge of western Lake Superior. As he prowled around the site, Douglas counted forty buildings.

Fort William, August 10, 1819

Dear Papa,

I hope this letter finds you well. I've had the most extraordinary journey to my first posting in a gigantic canoe paddled by *voyageurs*. I learned to paddle, too, but found the portaging hard. I am grateful to you for improving my French before I came. Everyone remarks on how well I speak the language.

Fort William is like a village arranged inside a rectangular palisade of thick wooden posts, nearly twelve feet [four metres] high with sharpened points on top. Over the fortified gate and at one corner overlooking the lake are bastions — lookouts with cannons where defenders can fight off attacks, though I doubt they've been needed. There's not much around here.

Outside are fields, some of oats and others for grazing, and by the wharf is a shipyard. Inside the palisade are huge storehouses, a vegetable garden, a smithy, an apothecary shop, a cooperage, and the counting house. Even a jail! All the buildings are constructed of peeled, squared logs. The senior officers

Fort William, the centre of the North West Company's commercial empire, circa 1811. Painting by Robert Irvine.

have comfortable residences, and there are log cabins for staff, traders, and visitors. I have a room in one of these. The Great Hall, for meals and meetings, separates the two main residences, and the kitchens and servants' quarters lie beneath.

On entering the hall I was excited to see a huge map of the North West Company's empire. David Thompson, the explorer and geographer, drew it to scale and finished it five years ago after two years' continual work. The map covers an entire wall and shows far more features than the map you gave me. The routes are one of the

company's secrets. I plan to study it closely. Now
I start my first job as an apprentice clerk in the
counting house and learn the fur trade business.

More later when I have settled in. I have
also sent a copy of this to Mama.

Your affectionate son,
James

Douglas joined Fort William in its busiest season and
scarcely had time to shake hands with the man in charge,
Dr. John McLoughlin, before he was put to work. Brigades
poured in from the north and the west, laden with furs, and
more arrived from Lachine carrying supplies until about three
thousand people were camped in and around the fort. The pork-
eaters slept under their canoes, the northmen who wintered in
the wilderness crawled into their battered tents, and the Native
guides and interpreters found refuge in their wigwams. Chatter
filled the air as old friends caught up with news, and lively
celebrations broke out everywhere as men let off steam.

Frenzied activity filled the fort from dawn to dusk and
sometimes late into the night as the brigades exchanged pelts
for supplies to get them through the coming winter in remote
forts. Untrained at that point, Douglas did his duty counting
bales, while the experienced clerks kept track of everything in
the counting house.

The huge summer gathering was also the annual Rendezvous
— NWC's version of a modern-day company convention. The
partners and senior officers held meetings to plan the year ahead,
decided promotions and postings, and talked with the traders
from every outpost. Douglas met the key players in the company

that summer — an important opportunity few apprentices experienced so early in their careers. The Rendezvous concluded with a wild party — bagpipe and fiddle music filled the Great Hall, and everyone danced with gusto until the first rays of sun streaked Lake Superior.

Long into the summer nights the after-dinner discussions and stories enthralled Douglas as he absorbed the unfamiliar culture. He learned for the first time of the bitter competition for furs between the Nor'westers and HBC men, which often flared into outright hostility. His jaw dropped on hearing about an ambush that had occurred while he was sailing into Quebec City. Bay men had captured several Nor'westers on a lengthy portage around the Grand Rapids on the Saskatchewan River and spirited them away to York Factory on Hudson Bay. No one knew the outcome yet.

Soon the brigades with the longest journeys paddled away in their smaller *canots du nord*, and later the *mangeurs de lard* left for Lachine. Every fur bale contained seventy beaver pelts, each bale worth a small fortune. By mid-October, all the temporary visitors had departed and calm descended. Douglas and the few dozen employees tackled the fort's backlog of paperwork.

As the new apprentice clerk, he was the youngest member of the staff at Fort William and began his training in the counting house. He learned NWC's inventory control, record-keeping that tracked all the pelts, trade goods, and supplies, and quartermaster duties in the trading post — tasks that quickly taught him how the company and a fort operated.

As the snow flew, Douglas heard the full story of the capture of Fort William, only three years before. He sat spellbound, his eyes round, as he thrilled to a prospect of excitement he hadn't anticipated.

"Well, it all started with Lord Selkirk," one trader said. "After marrying an heiress with shares in HBC, he sponsored a civilian settlement at Red River in 1811. He'd persuaded HBC that the new settlement could assist in stopping NWC from trading in the region."

"The first settlers Selkirk recruited nearly starved that first hard winter," another interjected. "They would have had it not been for the local Métis."

"Who are Métis?" James asked.

"They're people of mixed European and Indian blood."

James's ears pricked up — perhaps he wasn't so different, after all.

"We and the Métis were under no illusion about Selkirk's plans," the first man continued. "The Métis were furious over the loss of some of their land to his settlement and expected Selkirk to take more. We, the Nor'westers, feared his next move would be to block our trade route to deny passage of our furs and supplies. We feared we might starve if he did that."

"Did he?"

"Selkirk certainly tried. We hated him and suspected he was behind all manner of troubles we ran into. The Métis joined forces with us to oppose Selkirk and his plans, and we had to protect ourselves and our trade." The speaker sipped his whisky. "It came to a head in June 1816 when a band of Métis and a few Nor'westers rode past the HBC's fort. The governor of the settlement chased them with an armed escort and tried to force them to submit to Selkirk's authority. They refused. The confrontation escalated into a gunfight, and the Métis murdered the governor and twenty others."

"It's known as the Seven Oaks Massacre," the second trader added. "Selkirk was in Montreal when it happened. He retaliated by marching on Fort William with a force of mercenaries and captured it."

James suddenly realized the importance of bastions. "What happened then?"

Dr. McLoughlin took up the tale. "Selkirk arrested me, Simon Fraser, several senior partners of the company, and others. He took us to Montreal for trial. On the way a violent storm overtook us and nine prisoners drowned. So, in a twist of fate, it was Selkirk who went to trial, not us. He was charged with the responsibility for the drowning deaths, and we were released."

Douglas couldn't sleep that night.

Another piece of news disturbed him. NWC was clearly suffering severe financial problems. The fighting with HBC had always been expensive, but it was NWC's extended supply lines, as much as seven thousand kilometres from remote areas, and a sharp drop in demand for furs that were crippling the company. Indeed, the situation was so uncertain in 1819 that Douglas heard the company's shaky future raised after every dinner during the Rendezvous. McLoughlin told anyone who would listen that he thought the only answer was prompt amalgamation of the two trading companies. Spirited debate raged over that opinion well into the winter.

Douglas pondered the future. Perhaps his job wasn't as secure as his father had believed. Worried, he took up his pen to sort out his thoughts, at least when his ink wasn't frozen.

Fort William, January 15, 1820

After the scorching summer here, I can't believe the winter. When gales blow from the lake, they bring blizzards that last for days. It feels colder when it's windy. The snow is already halfway up the windows of my log house, and I'm to expect more storms until the end of April. The lake has frozen so thickly that a house could sit upon it and not fall through. Yesterday it was sunny but, oddly enough, it's colder when the sun shines than when it snows. I watched water, tipped from a bucket, freeze as it hit the ground a week ago. Nothing stirs outside. I have to wear gloves to work on the ledgers and am only truly warm by the fire in the mess hall.

Papa was right. Boredom is the real enemy. I can't go for walks, and I'm running short of books. Soon all I'll have left to read will be my Bible. I must devise some projects to fill my time and mind. Perhaps Thompson's map?

In the dark of the night I sometimes fear I won't be able to survive this apprenticeship for six years. The climate is so harsh and the remoteness from any kind of civilization is difficult to bear. I'm told it is far, far worse the farther west and north you go — there is no bread or butter to eat once you leave here, for other forts have no cows or grain. My idea that the fur trade would be an adventure was a dream. It is harder than I thought possible to live in this empty, freezing land.

Here I dream of the palm trees and warmth of Guiana. Last summer, amid the blackflies, I dreamed of the cool mists of Scotland. Perhaps when I stop dreaming it will mean I've adjusted.

I wonder if Papa truly understood where he was sending us.

In my most miserable moments I want to give this up and go home. But then I would have to pay back the company — I have no money of my own until I finish the six years, and I couldn't possibly ask Papa for it. If the company goes bankrupt, my problems would be over, but I don't really want this to happen, either. I wish I could discuss my dilemma with someone. Perhaps I should wait a while longer.

Before spring breakup, Douglas's patience rewarded him with an answer. He committed himself fully to the fur trade and decided to work hard for the duration of his apprenticeship, just as his father had taught him.

McLoughlin watched the process without intervening, having seen it many times. He recognized when his clerk's struggles ended and privately applauded Douglas's new resolve.

6

Postings and Promotions

John McLoughlin and James Douglas worked closely during the winter of 1819–20. The chief trader found his apprentice was a willing and rapid learner, as well as loyal. He grew to trust his work and gave him more responsibility. For his part Douglas appreciated the opportunity, and the two men, one white-haired and the other barely shaving, grew to like and respect each other. Their developing relationship was to have a lasting influence on Douglas's career. As the young clerk's first year with NWC drew to a close, McLoughlin decided he was ready for a promotion. The chief trader selected a small trading post called Île-à-la-Crosse (in today's northern Saskatchewan) for his protege so he would gain experience the fur trade.

"I'll show you where Île-à-la-Crosse is," McLoughlin said. "Let's look at the map." In the Great Hall he pointed out the fort to Douglas.

"How long does it take to get there?" Douglas asked.

"About two months. This is the route." Standing on a chair in front of Thompson's masterpiece, McLoughlin traced it with his finger as far as he could reach, moved the chair over, and continued showing Douglas the waterways the brigades followed. "It's a much harder journey than the one you did last year."

Secretly, in his spare time, Douglas painstakingly copied Thompson's map into an unused notebook. He filled the pages with carefully drawn sections, making sure he named every geographical feature and fort. The task took him a long time to complete. When he was done, he wrapped the notebook tightly in oilcloth and hid it at the bottom of his duffle, planning to add to it as he travelled.

In July the new HBC governor of Rupert's Land, George Simpson, passed through Fort William on his way to the Athabasca District (in present-day northern Alberta/Saskatchewan). Douglas met him briefly at a dinner rippling with undercurrents of dislike on both sides. Packing his map and his few possessions for his new posting didn't take long, and a few days after Simpson left, Douglas joined a brigade heading in the same direction.

Cumberland House, August 15, 1820

I had mixed feelings on departure — sorry to leave Fort William where I felt at home but anticipating trading with the Indians. I have been too tired to write on the trail. This second journey is three times as far as my first and over terrain that changes as the brigade speeds northwest. The canoes are narrower and faster, built for narrower waterways, and are paddled by only four or five *hommes du nord* who wear Native buckskin shirts and leggings, topped by a hooded coat in winter. These "northmen," the best being hardy Scots and Orkneymen, winter in the forts because a 4,350-mile [7,000-kilometre] round trip from Athabasca to Fort William can't be completed in the ice-free months of one summer. The *voyageurs* view themselves as vastly superior to the younger *mangeurs de lard*, boasting at every opportunity of their exploits and strength. Much of what they say is true.

I survive on pemmican, wild rice, and occasionally fish and game when the hunting is good. I'm learning to ignore hunger. The Nor'westers depend on the Indians' concentrated mixture of fat and dried meat for energy and trade mostly knives and cloth to get sufficient quantities. I hate the short northern nights when the brigade pushes on until twilight — we often travel sixteen hours a day. The workload on this journey is cruel, with more white water and many more back-breaking portages. The worst section lay around the cataracts on the Winnipeg River at Rat Portage, north from Lake of the Woods. This is the point at which the northmen say the west begins. The winter inactivity had reduced my stamina, and I was sore and tired until I toughened up.

I am discovering how important Indian women are to our comfort and safety —

along the way they repair tears in our canoes' birchbark hulls with tree roots and spruce gum, and supply us with moccasins. I traded a cooking pot for three pairs when my shoes wore out. Not only do they make pemmican, but also our snowshoes.

The ever-present risk of ambush by Bay men means we all carry rifles, and I take my turn on watch for a couple of hours every night, losing the rest my body craves. At Lake Winnipeg we raced other brigades north over 180 miles [300 kilometres] up the windy lake to Grand Rapids. We were on edge for the two-league (ten-kilometre) Grand Rapids portage around a narrow gorge where the ambush had occurred last year. With nerves twitching and eyes scouring the bush for any sign of trouble, we made it unmolested. I was both excited and frightened.

Douglas's brigade had unknowingly overtaken Simpson's party, so were ahead of their rivals. Simpson, equally unsure of the Nor'westers' location, armed his men to the teeth for the portage, expecting trouble at any moment. The rivals never did clash despite their proximity, but remained on high alert as they paddled furiously up the Saskatchewan River to Cumberland House, the first NWC fort built to challenge HBC's monopoly.[1]

While the brigade took a respite there, Douglas enjoyed the hospitality of this post's chief trader, William Connolly, and his Swampy Cree wife. Here Douglas began to realize how many Nor'westers of European ancestry had married Native women and had mixed-race children. It made him feel more comfortable with his origins than he had since he started school. No one out in the wilds seemed to notice his dark skin, and if they did, they didn't care.

After a short stay at Cumberland House, the brigade tackled the last stretch to Fort Île-à-la-Crosse in worsening weather. They arrived on September 6, soaked through, eight weeks after leaving Fort William. Douglas had grown out of his clothes once since leaving Scotland and had done so again, so he went to the stores and found new ones that fitted his almost two-metre-tall frame. He had piled on muscle during the 1,800 kilometres and was proud of his increased strength and stamina.

Simpson reached HBC's Fort Superior, just across the river, later the same day. Eyeball to eyeball, tension crackled between the rival forts' inhabitants. Fed by all the stories he had absorbed, the teenage Douglas was spoiling for a fight. He had a serious argument with a Bay guide — an older man with a reputation for brawling and winning. Despite warnings from others, Douglas challenged him to a duel. Fit from the journey and impetuous, Douglas neither lost nor won when the duel ended in a bloodless draw. Reprimanded by the chief trader in charge of the fort, he didn't do it again. However, he was the ringleader when the Nor'westers started holding "military parades" to provoke the HBC men across the river.

Although Île-à-la-Crosse was small in comparison to Fort William, it was a vital link in the transportation system of the NWC. It lay at a crossroads where the routes from Athabasca in the north and the Columbia River in the far west met. The brigades passed through in both directions in a steady stream during the summer months, keeping Douglas busy. This provided the opportunity to renew his acquaintance with the chief factors and traders of the company he had met at the annual

The forts at Île-à-la-Crosse, 1820. Left: Hudson's Bay Company's Fort Superior; right: North West Company's Fort Île-à-la-Crosse across the river. Painting by George Back.

Rendezvous. At Île-à-la-Crosse, Douglas started to understand the art of negotiation — how to trade for furs.

The Cree and Chipewyan, like all the First Nations peoples, trapped in the fall and spring every year. Since they had no use for money, they "sold" the pelts for goods they needed. Items in highest demand were metal knives and axes, which held their edge better than flint; guns and ammunition for easier hunting; and cooking utensils, cloth, and blankets. Douglas quickly discovered they drove a hard bargain and learned vital survival skills from them.

During the winter of 1820–21, though, events at the highest levels of NWC and HBC were reaching a climax. Douglas was unaware of the situation at the time, but the outcome would have a profound effect on his career. In England, after months of politicking and negotiation, the rivals finally came to terms and announced in late March 1821 that the two companies would amalgamate on June 1.

It took months for the news to filter through to the far-flung posts, but Douglas heard about the development before most Nor'westers from George Simpson, HBC's energetic governor who had a reputation for meanness. Simpson had arrived in Île-à-la-Crosse in June on an inspection tour of the forts HBC had acquired prior to making cuts in the operation. Douglas listened as Simpson informed the NWC men of the merger, antagonizing everyone by saying how disappointed he was that HBC's "opponents have not been driven out of the field."[2]

The Nor'westers responded to Simpson's words with anger. A stroke of a pen had betrayed their proud identity, and they perceived they had lost everything they had explored at great cost — the Athabasca, the Columbia, and the Mackenzie regions, as well as the finest beaver country on the continent, the land west of the Rockies called New Caledonia. True, the name of the North West Company disappeared and the proud *voyageurs* never paddled to and from Fort William again but, in fact, it was the vast NWC territories and the organization's better relationships with First Nations people that saved both failing firms. The Nor'westers also injected the stagnant HBC with new blood and provided routes through the Rockies. Even so, switching loyalty to the hated English competitor took time. Some never managed the transition, but Douglas sucked it up. Both he and other Nor'westers rightly feared HBC's larger and more complex bureaucracy — they believed their pay would drop and jobs would be lost. Douglas worried about his job, too, especially since he had actively incited Bay men so recently.

Simpson, leading the amalgamation, wasted no time in inspecting Fort Île-à-la-Crosse, eager to find irregularities and incompetence in its operation. Douglas, concealing his anxiety over his foolish duel and "parades," took the brunt of Simpson's inspection of the accounts and company records as the governor sought evidence of mismanagement. Douglas need not have worried. His attention to detail had everything in perfect order, and Simpson acknowledged as much. Douglas wasn't out of a job, just employed by another company as a clerk, second class. Eleven hundred other Nor'westers weren't so lucky — they didn't survive Simpson's ruthless downsizing. More important for Douglas, someone who mattered in the new hierarchy now knew something of his capabilities.

Douglas, recalling his father's wisdom to "behave properly" at all times, gave up his teenage antics. Over the next three years he grew in stature, skills, and knowledge and became more serious and intense. He learned to ice-fish and snowshoe and how to drive a dog team. His boss at Île-à-la-Crosse, George

Keith, watched the changes as Douglas matured, and like McLoughlin at Fort William, increased his responsibilities. Keith gave him opportunities to trade alone. The more positive feedback Douglas received the better he performed.

By 1823, when only twenty, Douglas was competent and sensible enough for Keith to leave him in charge of the fort for two weeks. During the summers of 1823 and 1824, Keith put Douglas in command of a Cree trading post on the English River called Poule d'eau Lake where he began to develop his understanding of aboriginal culture and character. On both occasions Douglas traded well and earned a reputation of fairness with the Natives.

Douglas's brother, Alexander, showed up in Île-à-la-Crosse in 1824, the only time their paths crossed, but James was away. Alexander waited around but had to leave for York Factory to sign off his indenture without seeing his brother. James was sorry he missed him, but lost no sleep over it. Alexander had performed poorly throughout his apprenticeship, mainly because he never adjusted to the rigours of the fur trade or was bright enough. He sailed back to Great Britain in the fall of 1824 and dropped out of sight. Whether the two brothers ever corresponded before or after this episode is a mystery.

One day in August 1824 someone else canoed into Île-à-la-Crosse whom Douglas greeted with real pleasure. The visitor was Dr. John McLoughlin, his mentor from Fort William. It was an important reunion. Not only did they renew their friendship, but McLoughlin measured up Douglas's progress.

The older man realized how much Douglas had grown up — he was tall and broad-shouldered from all the physical labour his work demanded. Douglas's facial features had matured, too. His wavy jet-black hair curled over his ears framing chiselled features, and his dark eyes were clear and purposeful. Douglas was handsome. But the most obvious change was his increased confidence. McLoughlin was delighted that the youngster had fulfilled his promise.

"Simpson promoted me at the annual council meeting," McLoughlin told Douglas as they talked after dinner. "Now I'm in charge of the Columbia District."

"Are you on your way to Fort Vancouver [on the Columbia River] or are you going somewhere else?"

"No, straight to Oregon country, though I'll visit what forts I can on the way."

"I wish I could go out west with you where the weather's warmer. The winters here are miserable and travel is hard."

"Ah, well, you'll have to serve out your apprenticeship before you get posted to a district headquarters."

Douglas swallowed his disappointment. At least he had tried.

McLoughlin made no promises to Douglas prior to leaving, but he certainly tucked him into the back of his mind for swift career progression within his Pacific Northwest territory.

At the age of twenty-three Douglas moved on again to an even smaller fort. Keith knew that the Athabasca region was in need of clerks and thought Douglas would benefit by serving there until his expected promotion came through that summer. So Douglas's posting to Fort Vermilion (in today's northern Alberta) was only temporary, but as always he was curious to see a new part of the country. He consulted his Thompson map, and with one Native as his guide, he willingly set off in early April 1825. They travelled the seven hundred kilometres on horseback and slept in tents. The two men hugged the banks of Churchill Lake to the headwaters of the Churchill River, turned northwest, and paused at Fort Chipewyan on Lake Athabasca, the hub of the Athabasca district. Then they followed the great Peace River west to Fort Vermilion. The chief factor's residence, the Old Bay House that Douglas knew well, still stands on the banks of the river amid grassy prairie. Douglas relished the change to big skies and open country where he saw his first bison.

In September, Douglas renewed his acquaintance with William Connolly when the latter's westbound brigade dropped into Fort Vermilion. They had met briefly at Cumberland House when Douglas was seventeen. Connolly was returning to Fort St. James from the annual council meeting on Hudson Bay and brought news of Douglas's next appointment.

7

Over the Shining Mountains

William Connolly not only passed along James Douglas's new posting but also the details of major changes taking place in the operation of HBC's westernmost territories. Douglas, no longer worried about his job, optimistically hoped the new developments might actually assist his career.

Governor Simpson had been enthusiastically implementing his plans to improve profitability now that HBC had the benefit of the North West Company's forts in the west. Their distance from the eastern collection centres had been difficult, if not impossible, to manage effectively and wore down those who had to travel back and forth. Simpson had devised an ambitious resolution. He was closing the less-profitable forts; arranging resupply of the western forts from the west by ships sailing around Cape Horn, rather than by brigades travelling overland from the east; and creating a separate western operation led from

Fort Vancouver, independent of York Factory on Hudson Bay.

"You've been posted to New Caledonia, part of the Northern Department," Connolly told Douglas as they sipped port after dinner. "I'm the chief factor there now. It's north and west of the Thompson River — it goes quite far north. The rivers and lakes teem with trout and salmon, our staple food. Magnificent country west of the Rockies. Lots of snow."

"Am I to come with you or follow later?" Douglas asked his new boss.

"Pack tonight. You'll be wintering at Fort McLeod, northeast of Fort St. James."

Douglas left Fort Vermilion the next day with Connolly's brigade after a sleepless night completing an inventory of the post and studying his precious map. His heart beat faster at the thought of crossing the mountains he had heard about and imagined for years. Once again Douglas was in the right place at the right time. Had he been at Île-à-la-Crosse he wouldn't have journeyed with Connolly and got to know him.

Fort St. James, November 15, 1825

My journey with Connolly's brigade proved difficult. We battled nasty weather — strong winds and even snow as we fought upstream against the Peace River's fast current to Rocky Mountain Portage House [now Hudson's Hope]. We negotiated a sixteen-mile [twenty-five-kilometre] portage where Indians, in large numbers, assisted us.

When the clouds broke, my first impression of the Shining Mountains, as the Indians call the Rockies, was awe-inspiring. They tower into the sky, capped with snow and filled with glaciers. Quite splendid! They left me thinking we would never find a way through. We did, of course, but it took an immense effort to get the brigade over them.

I was intrigued the day I saw all the streams begin to flow to the west. I had reached the Continental Divide for the first time in my life! It was an impressive moment, but no one else noticed. The travel continued perilous and fatiguing down the Parsnip, and my days were filled with adventures. I marked my Thompson copy with many notations.

Six weeks later I stood on the very spot [140 kilometres north of Prince George] where nineteen years ago Simon Fraser founded the first trading post west of the Rockies for NWC when he was exploring a route to the Pacific Ocean.[1] My first sight of McLeod Lake was very beautiful — filled with reflections in its still waters edged with ice.

I had expected to be at McLeod Lake, Trout Lake according to the Indians, for a year. However, on the journey Connolly decided he wanted me for himself. He announced the change in plan after we arrived. I'm happy to be going to the main fort, fifty-six miles [ninety kilometres] away. It's bigger and headquarters for New Caledonia, the name Fraser coined for this land.

We arrived at Fort St. James at the south

end of Stuart Lake on November 12. Fraser was responsible for establishing this post, too. Connolly told me how abundant and lustrous the furs are in this region and warned me of the dangers from bears. The fort has a spectacular view down the lake. Much of this area is unexplored and unmapped.

After an absence of nearly eight months, Connolly had only four days before he set out to find the best route to Fort Vancouver for the brigades the following spring. His wife and children were pleased to see him but unhappy that he had to leave again. Such is life in the fur trade!

Douglas settled into the winter routine and got to know Connolly's family better. In addition to his work as senior clerk, he was responsible for ensuring sufficient fresh food was available for the residents during the winter and spring by employing Native hunters. Self-sufficiency was difficult in New Caledonia, and gathering enough food consumed everyone, including Douglas. He ice-fished much of the first winter, returning his catches by dogsled. He also prepared the year-end report for Connolly before heading back to Fort McLeod on snowshoes with a sled of fish and other essentials.

Connolly called Douglas into his quarters one day in spring to discuss the younger man's future. Douglas, nearing the end of his apprenticeship, could scarcely believe how the time had flown. "I'm expecting you to sign on for three years now that you're free to do so," Connolly said. "If you do, you'll get a strong recommendation from me."

Father of British Columbia

"I definitely plan to stay," Douglas cheerfully reassured him.
"Then you can look forward to a promotion."

Douglas hoped it would be with John McLoughlin.

Connolly reported to HBC that his clerk could be relied upon to display common sense and responsibility under duress, and he had developed the necessary physical and mental strength to handle the hazards and rigours of the wilderness. Then he signed Douglas's new contract ahead of time, knowing he would be away with the brigade when it came into effect.

The only disappointment for Douglas that spring was remaining at the fort instead of joining the southbound brigade. The night before departure as the last canoes loaded, Connolly finally included Douglas since he was short of experienced personnel. Douglas was overjoyed, for it was another opportunity to demonstrate his mettle and visit McLoughlin. Besides, he was keen to see the Columbia District. He kept his elation in check as he carefully tucked the Thompson map among his clothes in his bag.

Next morning, May 5, 1826, two brigades left Fort St. James headed in different directions — one went east to York Factory and the other to Fort Vancouver. The weather was initially unkind. Late snow provided slippery, unpleasant conditions.

The southerly brigade travelled down the Stuart and Nechako rivers to join the Fraser at Fort George (today's Prince George). The mighty river was in freshet, swollen with spring run-off, and flowing high and fast. For Douglas it was a sight to behold. "Courage, *mon ami!*" he said to himself as the brigade moved into the current.

Immediately, the surge grabbed the laden canoes with a fierce hand. The river squeezed into a canyon a quarter of its width. The water squirted through, turning a sharp corner by a vertical cliff, and then poured into three channels around some islands. Douglas, who had heard stories of Simon Fraser's near loss here, gasped when he glimpsed a patch of seething water with gigantic standing waves in one channel. The canoes tore down another, the spray whistling past the crew's ears. Soaked through and breathless, the brigade dried out at a beach below as their heart rates slowed to normal.

June 24, 1826

We arrived at Fort Vancouver a couple of days ago and discovered the ship from London had arrived very late. Our men have had to assist with the unloading.

This journey was different from any I have done so far. Once past the canyon in the north, the brigade made fast time to the benchlands around Fort Alexandria where the river is wide. Here we switched the bales onto packhorses. This fort maintains a supply of horses for transport because Fraser's River below that point is too dangerous for canoes, laden or otherwise.

Our cavalcade rode overland to reach Fort Kamloops on May 23 where we found more horses. Connolly announced a day's rest. Then the Fort St. James brigade saddled up with those from other districts to ride south along the western shore of Okanagan Lake and down through desert country beside the Okanagan River until it joins the Columbia at Fort Okanogan. I have never seen desert before. The land is pale, the soil is sandy, and the plants have grey-green leaves. Men say there are rattlesnakes, but I did not see any.

Fort Okanogan is the gathering point for all the furs from New Caledonia and the Thompson, and through which all supplies pass going north. It is a typical HBC structure. This fort is so important it has light cannon for defence.

Here the brigades transferred into big boats, leaving the horses for the return journey, and we sailed into Fort Vancouver forty-three days after we left our northern home. It is high summer in Oregon Country and hot. The countryside not only looks different; it smells different. I like it very much and am enjoying fresh bread and butter again. Also, I will buy more books, new pens, and some ink.

Unloading the cargo from the ship took ten days. The brigade then laboured for another week sorting the supplies into "outfits," which would go to each post, and repacking them into forty-kilogram bales. Douglas managed to squeeze in some time with McLoughlin, but got no hint of new job opportunities.

The ship's late arrival had cost Connolly's brigade three weeks. The journey north was harder — the stretches in canoes meant paddling upstream, the temperatures soared, and there were insufficient packhorses for their greater loads at Fort Okanogan. Problems plagued the brigade all the way home, and it became a journey from hell.

On September 23, almost a month late, the brigade wearily trooped into Fort St. James eager for respite, only to find calamity awaiting them. Three summer salmon runs had failed and those who remained at the fort for the summer were starving and had almost given up on the brigade. That night the hungry residents ate well for the first time in weeks.

Fort St. James, March 15, 1827

I had no opportunity to rest after the gruelling five-month effort I had just endured — the outfits we hauled north had to go to the other posts immediately before winter set in. Connolly sent me to resupply Fort Fraser, near the east end of Fraser Lake, thirty miles [fifty kilometres] away, and to share being in charge with another clerk over the winter.

Despite roaming long distances to trade for furs and salmon in many aboriginal villages, the salmon proved scarce everywhere. I secured barely enough to last till now, let alone through the summer. The constant search for food meant I could not fully enjoy the trumpeter swans that rest here on their annual migrations. However, I did return to Fort St. James a couple of days ago with the best return of furs of any of the satellite forts. I am earning a reputation as a good trader, and I find it comes naturally.

Connolly restationed Douglas at the new fort on Bear Lake (about eighty-five kilometres due east of Fort St. James) for the summer of 1827. Whether his chief factor saw hints of a growing attraction between Douglas and his daughter, Amelia, and wanted to keep them apart is possible, for he had promised her to another. Douglas trekked to Bear Lake as ordered, of course, but missed the trip south to Fort Vancouver that year and may have missed Amelia, as well. Bear Lake was wonderful in the warm summer days. Douglas swam from its sandy beaches and enjoyed hiking around other nearby lakes and along the willow-lined Crooked River, another important water route. He spent most of his time trading for furs and caught as many fish as he could carry for the main fort. When he got back there, he learned that HBC had merged the New Caledonia, the Thompson River, and the Columbia Districts into one huge Columbia Department.

The salmon failed to return again that year, and the deprivation not only for Fort. St. James but all the posts in New Caledonia was more severe than the year before. To avert disaster Connolly sent Douglas on yet another fishing expedition to Yokogh Lake, while he went to Babine Lake where the trout and char grew big and fat. Douglas returned at the beginning of November with over nine thousand whitefish that enabled the fort to support everyone for the winter if rationed carefully. A boring diet, certainly, but nutritious.

Fort St. James, January 2, 1828

> I am very weary with all the fishing and travelling in such grim conditions. The sustainability of forts here is very questionable and too much energy is devoted to survival. The spectre of starvation is very real.
>
> The isolation and lack of books is getting me down. I want a respite and a promotion out. If the latter does not come soon, I will not renew my contract.

8

Un mariage à la façon du pays

The past winters' privation and bitter weather, relentless fatigue, and constant worry had dissolved James Douglas's enthusiasm for the fur trade. When the hoped-for posting out of New Caledonia didn't materialize, he decided not to extend his contract with HBC. At twenty-four a little comfort and relaxation after eight years in the wilderness tempted him sorely. But he hadn't reckoned with his chief factor. Connolly didn't want to lose his best employee and urged him to sign on again, offering to boost his yearly salary from £60 to £100.

But was it this offer that caused Douglas to change his mind? Was it Amelia? Or did Connolly sweeten the pot by offering him Amelia's hand in marriage? It wasn't an unheard of method of persuasion, and marriages were often arranged for trade benefits with Native bands. Both Douglas and Amelia were of marriageable age; neither had many potential partners to choose from; and Douglas, who enjoyed robust health, was an excellent catch from a father's point of view.

But what was in it for him? Douglas wondered. Was he ready for marriage and children? Amelia was certainly comely, and she was used to the hardships of the fur trade life. He had no misgivings about her mixed race in a society where most white men wedded Native women. Douglas wondered briefly if Connolly had consulted his daughter before he made the offer. Ironically, it was Valentine's Day 1828 when the two men struck the deal and Douglas signed up for another three years with HBC — and a wedding.

Amelia had celebrated her sixteenth birthday on New Year's Day. Her mother, the daughter of a Swampy Cree chief, had married Connolly in 1803. Their first-born was John, and Amelia followed nine years later in 1812. She was a healthy baby and much cherished. Amelia was called a mixed-blood child by her Cree relatives, a half-breed by her father, and Métis by the *voyageurs*, but none of these descriptions were racial slurs. She grew up among other children of similar backgrounds and never gave hers a second thought.

Since Amelia's father spoke French at home and at work, and her mother spoke Cree, Amelia was bilingual by age three, but she didn't speak English. She was used to moving around — the family had followed Connolly from fort to fort, from the east to the far west, as he progressed through the ranks of the fur trade. She had spent her whole life surrounded by men and had known privation and danger.

By sixteen these experiences and her upbringing had made her inwardly strong and outwardly capable. She could skin animals for the pot and smoke salmon. Amelia was also shy and spoke slowly after much thought. Her nickname was "Little

Snowbird." "Little," because she was *petite*, and "Snowbird," because she had inherited light skin from her father. She wore her straight blue-black hair parted in the middle and pulled back. Her eyes were an unusual grey, her lips thin and straight.

After the deal was made, Douglas began a serious two-month courtship of Amelia, with the wedding planned for the end of April. Amelia needed no urging, and she welcomed Douglas's wooing. After all, he was handsome and the most eligible bachelor available, if somewhat lacking in humour. Three days before the wedding and a week before the brigade was to leave for Fort Vancouver, news of a murder arrived that nearly ruined both.

A company man had been murdered on his way to Babine Lake. HBC policy demanded harsh and immediate punishment for the perpetrators, and Connolly and Douglas wanted swift justice. Stress and anxiety escalated within the fort and outside it as Amelia made her final preparations to marry Douglas.

Fort St. James, April 28, 1828

> Dear Papa,
> I'm delighted to tell you that I am now married. Yesterday I wed Amelia Connolly, the daughter of the chief factor of New Caledonia. As there are no clergy within a thousand miles [1,600 kilometres], William, her father, performed the marriage for us. I asked him to use the Church of England service from the prayer book, and we both gladly spoke our wedding vows, but in French — I with a strong voice and Amelia more quietly. We call this *un mariage à la façon du pays*, which means "a

marriage in the custom of the country." This is how all marriages are performed here.

Everyone came to our wedding, even the Indian chiefs and their families. We were feasted and danced all night long to lively fiddle music. I hope you will wish us every happiness.

Your son,
James

Connolly placed the bridegroom in charge of New Caledonia before he departed with the brigade. He left with misgivings about the situation that faced Douglas concerning the murder, as well as anxiety in case the salmon failed again.

Douglas, eager to prove himself in command, lost no time in acting. His investigations soon determined that a young Native suspected of the murder, and accused of two previous killings, had sought sanctuary in the house of the chief of the Stuart Lake band. Douglas rounded up a group of men, and when Chief Kwah was away, entered his house. They dragged the suspect outside and beat him to death with a hoe, leaving the body where it fell.

In truth, Douglas had no proof their victim had been the killer involved in the Babine murder, but he was satisfied he had set an example that would deter further violence against HBC. However, entering a chief's house to apprehend someone sheltering inside was a serious breach of aboriginal culture, and Douglas should have known better. His misjudgment and precipitate actions caused untold heartache for him and everyone in the fort a few days later.

Infuriated upon his return to find the dead body outside

his house, Chief Kwah and his followers invaded the fort and captured Douglas, threatening to kill him. Douglas fought back with all his strength, yelling loudly as the Natives held him down on a table in the main hall. A crowd quickly gathered.[1]

The chief waited until Douglas exhausted himself and spoke for all to hear. Kwah agreed that the alleged killer had to die but reprimanded Douglas for doing the deed in a Native village. Had Douglas chosen to do it elsewhere, the chief said, he could have overlooked the slaying. As it was, he now had to compensate the dead man's family with supplies, which he expected Douglas to provide.

Douglas sharply refused, and more than once. The chief, knowing he had the upper hand, continued bargaining for clothing, food, axes, tobacco, and guns for the bereaved family and, no doubt, for his band, too. He browbeat Douglas until he gave in. Kwah released Douglas, and the latter donated the goods with bad grace. Other than his childish pranks at Île-à-la-Crosse, Douglas's poor handling of the murder was the only serious mistake he made during his career in the fur trade.

Unfortunately for Douglas, Governor Simpson met Chief Kwah in September during one of his whistle-stop visits and first heard about the confrontation from him. He was incensed over Douglas's handling of the affair and its likely negative effect on trade. Simpson decided to remove Douglas from the area when he realized the Natives' animosity toward his subordinate was widespread, but he didn't act immediately.

The Natives' resentment toward Douglas seethed for months and finally boiled over in November 1828. On the trail to Fraser Lake a pack of angry young band members attacked him. He escaped with his life only after displaying great courage in the face of death. Connolly reported this and other confrontations to Simpson, praising Douglas's bravery and emphasizing his safety in New Caledonia was at risk.

Fort St. James, November 12, 1829

The salmon returned in large numbers last summer while I was again in charge of Fort St. James during the brigade's journey to Fort Vancouver. I remained behind because Amelia was expecting our first child, a gesture from my father-in-law that I appreciated. So did Amelia. When he returned, he found the fort replete with dried salmon that I amassed by trading with the local Indian villages. This proved that most are willing to deal with me again after a long stretch of refusals.

I became a father for the first time two days ago when our daughter was born in the wee hours. We called her Amelia. I was lucky to have been home as I have been mostly away this fall delivering outfits and trading for fish and furs. The babe is healthy, and Amelia, though tired, is well, too.

9

Fort Vancouver in Oregon Country

In January 1830, James Douglas was getting ready for yet another fishing expedition to Babine Lake when a chief trader from York Factory arrived with a letter from George Simpson. Douglas smiled as he read: "You are to report to Fort Vancouver without loss of time to take up the position of accountant." It was his long-awaited ticket out — a big promotion for a man of only twenty-seven, and it was in Oregon Country.

The news was a blow to Connolly who would lose his best employee, but he understood how important the move was for his son-in-law. The news hit Amelia particularly hard, for baby Amelia was sick and unable to travel. Amelia had to be content with making the trip south with the brigade five months later.

Adding his dog-eared and stained Thompson map, extra clothing, and books to his already packed gear, Douglas prepared quickly. He was used to difficult farewells, but Amelia cried bitterly when he left Fort St. James on January 30, 1830, in a snowstorm. The slower winter travel afforded Douglas thinking time. Sitting in the saddle, lulled by the rhythm of the horse's motion along the Okanagan Valley, he looked back at his progress and planned his future. He rejoiced that he had finally made the critical turn toward a steady rise to senior HBC rank. By following his father's advice to work hard, he had achieved success young. Douglas also knew he had capitalized on being in the right place at the right time with men of influence and promised himself he would continue this practice.

Douglas was greatly cheered during the long journey by the prospect of life in the more civilized centre of western operations, which had a milder climate and no fishing expeditions. Working for John McLoughlin again, he knew, would be a pleasure. He arrived in springtime, just before the first supply ship from England docked.

Fort Vancouver, March 30, 1830

> Although I have been to Fort Vancouver before, I look with renewed amazement at the abundance of fresh food and the huge variety of supplies that greeted me after a decade of deprivation. Nearby farms, an orchard, vegetable plots, and cows, pigs, and sheep supplement a constant flow of goods from England and other countries. There will be no more hunger or bone-numbing winters, no more loneliness or fears of attack. It is like arriving in heaven.

> A new, bigger fort is under construction since I was here in 1826, and I learn we are entitled to a residence of our own. Amelia will

be delighted. I have missed her much and wish
it was worth writing to her, but she will arrive
before the letter can leave.

The territory of HBC's Columbia Department, west of the
Rockies, ran from Russian Alaska south to encompass all of the
Columbia River Basin known as Oregon Country. Great Britain
and the United States had agreed to joint occupation of the region,
but neither owned or governed it. In reality the Hudson's Bay
Company ruled the whole territory. In 1830 company employees
were the only individuals of European descent who lived there.

HBC's goal for the department had been twofold: secure more
furs and prevent its competitors, the Russians and the Americans,
from threatening its territory and profits. Colonization had never
been on HBC's agenda. In fact, the company actively opposed
the practice because settlers meant governments and that
meant loss of absolute control. Before Douglas arrived at Fort
Vancouver in 1830, threats to the Columbia Department had
eased. Negotiations in 1825 had fixed the Russian boundary at
54°N, and 1828 had seen the renewal of the Convention of Joint
Occupancy between Britain and the United States that again
deferred the worrying boundary issue west of the Rockies.

Douglas worked in Fort Vancouver during its golden age. The
fort lay 150 kilometres up the Columbia River on its north bank
in a strategic position to protect British interests. The big river was
navigable once ocean-going vessels negotiated the dangerous bar
guarding its mouth. McLoughlin had chosen a site that was flat
and fertile above the Columbia's flood plain where sturdy wharfs
could be constructed. All HBC forts aimed for self-sufficiency,
and this one approached that goal — Fort Vancouver had both
arable and dairy farms and its own sawmill — and benefited

from the abundance of salmon in the river. Douglas understood why everyone called the area *la jolie prairie*.

As he walked around the new fort, he realized its size and sophistication were quite unlike any he had seen since arriving in North America as an apprentice. As years of strain slipped from his shoulders, he knew he was going to enjoy living here. Although the fort had a stockade, it wasn't defended, and the forty buildings within included houses for the senior officers, a school, a chapel, a pharmacy, a smithy, and joy of joys, a library. Outside the fort were a small shipyard, additional housing, a tannery, a distillery, and a dairy. That night Douglas ate his first fresh bread and butter since he was last there. The next day he unpacked and carefully concealed his precious map below his shirts in a drawer in his new bedroom.

Fort Vancouver, April 10, 1830

> This fort is the largest non-Native settlement west of the Great Plains, and in addition to HBC personnel, has Hawaiians, Métis, and Native Americans, mostly Cree and Iroquois, living here. French is still the language of everyday affairs, but the trading language is Chinook, a mixture of many Native and non-Native tongues. All the company records, accounts, and journals are kept in English because of the need to send them to Great Britain for examination. Fort Vancouver manages thirty-four trading posts, twenty-four ports, and six hundred employees.

Douglas was busy, but not always happy.

10

Grief and Joy

Before Amelia joined him, James Douglas began to tease out the financial affairs of the huge operation so he could get up to speed. It meant many hours in the counting house before he felt he had a thorough grip on the enterprise.

At midsummer Douglas's eyes kept straying from the ledgers to the river as he watched for signs of the New Caledonia brigade. He longed for it to arrive, so he could show Amelia her new house. At last the boats came into view, and he hurried to the wharf. Soon he saw Amelia disembarking, then Connolly. But where was his daughter?

As his wife drew closer, Douglas took in her wooden face and lifeless eyes. His heart lurched. "What's wrong, my dear?"

Amelia's face crumpled, and tears poured down her cheeks as she clutched his arm. "We had a terrible winter. Amelia died."

Douglas put his arm around her, and with Connolly's help

guided his distraught wife to the house. He swallowed his disappointment at the joyless reunion and ignored his own upwelling of grief to let her pour out her sorrow and distress. When she could cry no more, Douglas heard the details. His father-in-law had fallen dangerously ill the day after he left, and their daughter had never recovered from her illness. Sobbing again, Amelia explained that little Amelia had died four weeks after she said farewell, and Connolly had been too ill to conduct the burial service. Now she had left her grave behind and would never see it again.

There was more. Amelia was missing her mother and siblings more acutely than she had expected and felt guilty that her mother would have to deliver an eleventh child without her. However, she couldn't tell Douglas the worst news of all.

Douglas learned that from his father-in-law. Connolly had had enough of the privations and difficulties in New Caledonia and was returning to Montreal with his family. Douglas tenderly comforted his wife who would likely never see her family again, drawing on how he had felt at nine with his first gut-wrenching separation. But he was suffering, too — he was quite unprepared for the loss of little Amelia. Only his wife saw his grief; in front of others he displayed no emotion.

McLoughlin's wife helped Douglas in his care of Amelia. Marguerite, more than twenty years Amelia's senior, was also the daughter of a Native woman and a European father. She spoke Cree and was the person who provided Amelia with a woman's sympathy, company, and guidance. Without a brood of children of her own, Amelia ate many lonely meals, at least initially, because of the HBC tradition that had the men dine together in the mess hall every night. Shyly, she learned her duties in a much larger community as the wife of a senior HBC employee.

Douglas anticipated that the climate, good food, and

Marguerite's friendship would bolster Amelia and ease her losses. Soon she was expecting their second child, which delighted them both. This time it was a boy, born in May 1831, whom Douglas named after his brother, Alexander. He was a healthy baby with a sunny disposition and was loved by everyone.

In the ensuing years McLoughlin regularly sent Douglas to York Factory on Hudson Bay for the annual council meeting to deliver the accounts of the previous year and receive the instructions for the next. Even using the York Factory Express route, it took four months to get there and four to return. He missed several summers in Oregon Country that way, but missed his beloved son more.

When Douglas left for York Factory in 1833, he was unaware that Amelia was pregnant. By the time he returned, he learned that a son, John, had been born and died. Amelia solemnly led Douglas through the trees outside the fort to the burial ground in a meadow where wildflowers bloomed in summer. At John's grave he mourned the child he had known nothing about.

McLoughlin sent Douglas to York Factory again in 1834, but recalled him after an employee fell ill at the fort. He returned to Amelia, who told him she was two months' pregnant, and to Alexander who was now three. Douglas, thrilled to be unexpectedly home, tossed his gurgling son into the air. Somehow the action hurt Alexander seriously, and a month later he was dead. United in grief again, Douglas and Amelia stood beside the grave as the lad's small coffin was lowered into the ground beside John's.

Amelia delivered twins, Cecilia and Maria, in October 1834, whom Douglas ensured were promptly baptized by a visiting Methodist minister. A few months afterward he left his family of three behind once more to undertake the longest journey of his life.

York Factory, July 20, 1835

My dear wife,

I hope you and the twins are well and are enjoying the summer in Fort Vancouver this year. I am fine and have much to tell you. I am sending this letter now via the Express so that the good news arrives before I do.

We encountered deep snow in the Rockies. Not only did I attend the Northern Council meeting in Fort Garry, but I also spent a month in meetings at York Factory. As I plan to return via Fort Assiniboine on the Athabasca River, this round trip is over five thousand miles [eight thousand kilometres]. I shall be away for nine months all told. It follows well-travelled routes and is less arduous than the journeys from Fort St. James. I am quite enjoying myself.

I am delighted to tell you that at Fort Garry, Simpson promoted me to chief trader. So I am one of only twenty-eight in HBC and a "commissioned gentleman." Now I have the right to participate fully in the council's decision-making processes, a long-held desire. I am the youngest trader at thirty. This promotion means I not only earn £400 a year, up from £100, but also a one-eighty-fifth share in the company's profits. With annual expenses of only £30, our savings will increase rapidly. With your agreement, I plan to send my sister, Cecilia, regular bank drafts and donate more to charity.

I am looking forward to being home with
you and the twins.

Your loving husband,
James

Governor Simpson had come to appreciate his "Scotch West Indian's" talents despite the misstep at Fort St. James. Simpson wrote in an assessment of Douglas that he was "a stout powerful active man of good conduct and respectable abilities. Tolerably well educated, expresses himself clearly on paper, understands our Counting House business and is an excellent Trader. Well qualified for any Service requiring bodily exertion, firmness of mind, and the exercise of good judgment, but furiously violent when roused."[1] The latter remark almost certainly refers to Douglas's actions after the murder at Babine Lake.

During this epic journey of 1834, Douglas resolved to use his notebooks more diligently, and they soon became a daily passion, if not an obsession. Now, years after his father taught him to jot down items of interest, he began to collect tidbits on an array of topics. His entries included the meanings of names, maps he drew, and facts about astronomy and Scottish history, to identify just a handful. Science, machinery, law, anthropology, and sociology intrigued him, too, and he continued to post entries until he died.

When Douglas got back to his family, a sorrowful walk to the cemetery marred another reunion. Amelia accompanied him to Maria's grave on his first day home. Out of four pregnancies and five live births, Douglas and Amelia had only one surviving child — Cecilia.

11

Leadership

Jamed Douglas's next few years as chief trader at Fort Vancouver sharpened his leadership skills. His time was filled with a series of journeys, some long, some short, punctuated with periods of working at home. These provided him with a string of opportunities for high-level negotiations, the management of conflicts and crises, and the implementation of new ideas. For Amelia the time meant getting pregnant most years and facing the spectre of death whenever a child was born.

The fort prospered and received more visitors each year bringing news and injections of civilization. Food was plentiful and life was pleasant. Douglas joined his wife occasionally for social events such as picnics, horseback rides, and canoe trips to local beauty spots. Usually, though, the women of the fort went on these expeditions without their partners, taking their children and enjoying one another's company.

The arrival in 1836 of some American clergy, their wives, and assorted missionaries was a big day for the residents of Fort Vancouver. McLoughlin formally welcomed them all and invited the visitors to stay at the fort. Church societies on the East Coast had sent them to convert the Natives and provide Christian worship for everyone. But one arrival was to stay — Governor Simpson had appointed Reverend Herbert Beaver, an Anglican priest from England, as chaplain to the Columbia Department. Douglas, who firmly believed in a Christian God, looked forward to the permanent ministry of an ordained cleric.

However, the visitors' haughty moral outlook and judgmental reaction to the HBC way of life on the frontier bewildered the Douglases and others. Inevitably, the unions between Native women and white men, none of which had been conducted in church, horrified the visitors. Their loudly voiced criticism especially hurt the women who took the brunt of their superior attitude and unkind words. Both the Douglases and McLoughlins breathed a collective sigh of relief when the missionaries departed to convert the Indians.

But it was Reverend Beaver who turned out to be the worst offender. He was quite unable to accept what living on the edge of the frontier really meant, and his incessant "holier-than-thou" disapproval drove everyone mad. When McLoughlin finally refused to speak with him anymore, Douglas inherited him as his burden. He ran interference and acted as an intermediary between his boss and Beaver. Surprisingly, Douglas didn't often get angry with Beaver. He managed to deal with the man's pettiness and unwillingness to adapt with uncharacteristic patience. Perhaps growing up in Scotland had instilled a respect for men of the cloth that was hard to discard.

Amelia gave birth to another daughter in November 1836 in the middle of a smallpox outbreak. Ellen was healthy at birth, which relieved her parents' anxiety. However, her arrival caused Douglas's first blazing row with Beaver after the cleric refused to baptize Ellen. Beaver told Douglas his marriage, performed in the "custom of the country," was invalid and his children were illegitimate, despite knowing that no clergy were available to perform his wedding. Douglas was deeply hurt by Beaver's accusation, but also feared he might have done something immoral since Amelia had already given birth to six children. Because Douglas took his Christian faith seriously, he thought it through and decided he should set his relationship right from the church's point of view, as well as ensure his children didn't grow up illegitimate. He concluded that he and Amelia should remarry.

Amelia, who normally wouldn't have cared either way, found herself in an unexpected position after receiving troubling news about her parents in Montreal. After a gruelling journey across the country with his wife and six children, Amelia's father had recently married a former lover in Montreal after he convinced a Catholic priest his former *mariage à la façon du pays* was invalid. Amelia knew that her father's second marriage made her illegitimate and also demonstrated that her own first wedding could be questioned, leaving her children illegitimate, too. She felt the risks keenly and readily agreed to the second marriage ceremony.

Douglas approached this wedding with honest emotion, for he was both devoted and faithful to his wife. Amelia, pragmatic and in love with her husband, entered into the ceremony fully, too. Reverend Beaver united them in Holy Matrimony in February 1837, the first marriage he performed at Fort Vancouver. The chaplain then baptized Ellen.

In March, Douglas set out for York Factory and again had to turn back, so the family enjoyed the summer season together. But in November, Amelia and Douglas stood once more at a grave dug beside the three that belonged to John, Alexander, and Maria. Ellen had died unexpectedly of unknown causes, and Beaver performed the Anglican burial rite. Four of the Douglas babies now lay in the fort's cemetery. This wasn't an unusual infant mortality rate for the time and location, but was heartbreaking for the parents nonetheless. In the midst of the anguish over Beaver's narrow-mindedness, her parents' news, and Ellen's death, Amelia became pregnant. Hope filled their hearts again.

Fort Vancouver, June 10, 1838

I became acting chief factor for the Columbia Department when McLoughlin made a lengthy visit to England, an important opportunity to prove my leadership skills. I had expected it to come but not so soon. I am to be in command with all the demanding responsibilities for two years. My determination to succeed is matched by McLoughlin's confidence in me. He wrote saying how much he admired my ability and zeal, and appreciated my support and assistance.

Being chief factor is much like being the captain of a ship — total authority coupled with absolute responsibility for everything and everyone. I am still only thirty-five years old and keen to do it well.

Reverend Beaver's fanaticism continued as one of Douglas's leadership burdens. As his criticism became more strident and nasty, the well-being of the fort's residents and, indirectly, the business enterprise declined. The year before, and unknown to McLoughlin and Douglas, Beaver had penned a poisonous letter to HBC in London, denouncing the chief factor and his wife as well as the operation of the fort. When McLoughlin discovered a copy of the letter just before he left for London, he lost his temper and physically attacked Beaver. Later he fired him. Beaver's words had concerned McLoughlin's wife. The clergyman had inferred that Marguerite was McLoughlin's mistress and a prostitute. Douglas's role was to ensure that Beaver did no further damage and to see him off the premises.

However, Beaver didn't go quietly. He wrote another devastating report of forty-one pages to the London committee in which he suggested the fort used child labour and practised slavery, which the British Empire had abolished in 1833. The indictment also contained un-Christian condemnation of nearly everyone at Fort Vancouver, and though Douglas could hardly believe it, a recommendation that the women not legally married be denied food and medical care.

Douglas was beyond infuriated with the former chaplain but took up his pen, instead of his sword. He wrote to Beaver first and then to his London superiors. He told Beaver that his accusations against the wives in the fort were both malicious and slanderous. He informed HBC that there weren't and never would be prostitutes or slaves at Fort Vancouver and then provided suggestions about behaviour on the frontier: "A clergyman must quit the closet ... he must shun discord, avoid uncharitable feelings, temper zeal with discretion...."[1] In October 1838, Douglas couldn't bring himself to bid Beaver farewell when the chaplain sailed for England to continue his mischief. Life at the fort and trade quickly recovered, and Douglas conducted the Sunday services, something he enjoyed.

Douglas had matured into a man who thought deeply about complex social and political issues, who lived an honest and self-disciplined life, and whose compassion toward his fellow human beings guided his relationships. He never swore, even in male company; he drank little; he was always strict but fair with staff, which developed their respect; he treated the Natives with respect; and he cared about women's issues, children, and orphans, and gave generously to charity. Douglas was distinctly atypical for his era and for HBC. He had developed into a progressive "liberal" in an era of privileged right-wing attitudes, a man who vigorously upheld the unpopular positions he took. Racial discrimination was one such issue, and a personal one at that. Slavery was another, and he adamantly opposed it.

Fort Vancouver, October 7, 1838

> After the enactment of the Slavery Abolition Act of 1833, HBC had circulated a directive to abolish it whenever we found it. Slavery existed not within the forts but as part of many Native cultures with whom we traded.
>
> I eagerly took up the call, having long believed slavery was morally wrong, and endeavoured to encourage the Natives around Fort Vancouver to free their slaves voluntarily. Others used force to make Natives give up their slaves, but I preferred to follow a more peaceable path. To set a good example, I gave

a young runaway slave a job, while continuing my verbal persuasion of the Native chiefs and elders. When my efforts failed to have much effect, I had the difficult task of informing the London Committee of my lacklustre results. I chose my words carefully and wrote that not one person "residing in the fort" was a slave, but a free British subject.

12

Negotiator and Family Man

John McLoughlin returned late in 1839 to find James Douglas and Amelia with a new baby in the nursery. Jane was already seven months old and thriving. An itinerant Catholic priest had baptized her at Douglas's request — he preferred Father Modeste Demers's more inclusive theology to Herbert Beaver's stifling moral rectitude.

McLoughlin and Douglas had much to discuss and spent the next few days and nights catching up.

"You've done an outstanding job while I've been away," the chief factor said as they sat alone in the Great Hall. "Thank you. I'll give London the details and perhaps soon you'll get another promotion."

"I'd appreciate that, sir," Douglas said, savouring his port.

"The issue that most concerns London now is the increasing number of settlers finding their way to Oregon Country. I know the renewed Joint Occupancy Agreement of 1828 has provided the right of settlement, but HBC doesn't want an influx of settlers agitating for annexation to the United States."

"I know it would mean a loss of our power in the region, but in my judgment we're soon going to see a flood of settlers whatever HBC wants," Douglas said.

McLoughlin lapsed into silence and stared into the flames. Unknown to Douglas, he was musing about how he might benefit from a larger population.

Douglas filled the vacuum. "More settlers mean a form of government will surely follow, and if they're American settlers, the land certainly will become part of the United States, not Britain. And the decision on a boundary between British and American territory west of the Rockies will rise to the top of the agenda for both countries. What will we do if they decide to run it north of here along the forty-ninth parallel as it is in the East?"

"George Simpson's working to eliminate that possibility by expanding our operations here. That might help."

The two men discussed possible steps to preserve HBC territory as it was, and failing that, a fallback position. They decided, after getting further advice from London, to act as soon as possible. Then they went to bed.

The next day McLoughlin called Douglas into his office and shut the door. "Further to our discussions last night, the company has established a new subsidiary. It's called the Puget Sound Agricultural Company. London hopes it will be a negotiating tool in HBC's expansion into Alaska."

"How will that work?"

"Its farms' food and products will be offered to the Russian American Company posts in Alaska, but only if they agree to HBC's presence there. PSAC should deliver us a profit at the same time." McLoughlin paused. "I'm the first superintendent of the enterprise."

Douglas thought for a moment, then said, "As a commissioned gentleman, can I invest in PSAC?"

"Of course."

Douglas needed no further encouragement from his boss and put down £1,000 from his substantial savings. He was eager to invest now that he could afford it.

With McLoughlin back, Douglas pursued his work as chief trader of the Columbia Department more diligently. For several years he travelled widely on the west coast of North America, forming links with new trading partners as HBC diversified and conducting high-level negotiations for the company.

By 1840, Douglas was in his prime at thirty-seven years old — he was a canny trader, good with the Native tribes, a competent businessman, and a decisive leader attuned to the politics of the region and HBC. He undertook a six-month inspection tour that included negotiations with the Russians in Alaska, which were one of the steps he and McLoughlin had discussed to secure HBC's position. Douglas was to negotiate leases for several forts on the Alaska Panhandle in an effort to dominate control of the North Pacific fur trade.

The first leg of his journey was to Fort Nisqually on Puget Sound to meet his ship. Douglas showed presence of mind and personal courage when he rescued a man who had fallen into a fast-flowing, debris-clogged river. No one else had been brave enough to battle the freezing currents, which presented "a danger so appalling [it] daunted the boldest spirits."[1]

The party then boarded the SS *Beaver*, which gave Douglas his first opportunity to visit HBC forts accessible only by sea. They sailed north through Puget Sound and fifty kilometres up the Fraser River to Fort Langley. Steadily, the *Beaver* steamed northward, stopping at Comox on Vancouver Island where Douglas bought fifty beaver skins, and at Fort Simpson (now Port Simpson, north of Prince Rupert) for food and supplies. They called in at the Russians' Fort Stikine (Wrangell, Alaska) before coming alongside at Sitka.

Douglas conducted four days of historic meetings with the Russian governor. His dignity and confidence, and his years of learning to judge people, led to rapid success. He negotiated a lease for HBC of the entire Alaskan Panhandle in exchange for an annual payment of furs and an agreement to supply Russian posts with food and goods from the new subsidiary (PSAC). Although Douglas was outwardly friendly, he wasn't impressed with the Russian organization. However, he confined his negative opinions of the operation to his notebook.

He put the new deal into immediate effect at Fort Stikine, taking possession of it for HBC by raising the British flag and firing a seven-gun salute. The *Beaver* sailed north again to establish Fort Taku (today's Juneau). Its crew erected the typical HBC stockade and two bastions and supplied sufficient food and fuel to support a small staff for the winter.

On the long southward voyage, Douglas visited Fort McLoughlin (now Bella Bella), Texada Island, and Fort Langley again. He hadn't enjoyed the weather during the voyage — it had been rainy and cold most of the time, and the experience left him with an impression of gloomy, wet days and a forbidding coastline.

Flushed with the achievements of his six-month odyssey, Douglas arrived home in October to exciting news. HBC had promoted him to chief factor in recognition of his outstanding work on its behalf in Alaska. This advancement was surprisingly soon after his appointment as chief trader and occasioned some envy in others not so fortunate. His salary doubled overnight. Coming home meant he could enjoy his daughters again — Cecilia was now six and Jane, eighteen months old — because he missed them deeply when he was away.

But he wasn't home for long. On December 2 he headed to Alta (Mexican) California on another diplomatic mission before Christmas. This step of the HBC plan for dominance on the West Coast involved finding a site for a permanent HBC trading post, as well as gaining the right to trap furs and to trade on the Californian coast.

At Sea, December 29, 1840

> I boarded the *Columbia* at Fort George [Astoria] for the voyage south. Although I had lived on the river for a decade, I had never crossed the hazardous bar at the mouth of the Columbia River. The Pacific storms prevented the ship from attempting this dangerous manoeuvre for two weeks. When we did finally negotiate the bar safely, it was nearly Christmas. I found I wasn't as good a sailor on the north Pacific in winter as I had been on the Atlantic. This time I suffered persistent *mal de mer* [seasickness] and missed all the season's festivities except Divine Service.

Douglas gratefully reached dry land on the first day of 1841, and after putting on his best outfit, called upon the governor of Alta California on January 3 in Monterey, the capital. When Douglas first met Governor Alvaredo, he thought the man was cold and preoccupied, but the chief factor slowly thawed him out. Their discussions over three weeks became spirited.

Not all points went Douglas's way. He had to work hard at these negotiations. In the end he relinquished to the Mexicans the right to trap furs in the coastal valleys. HBC would, in future, have to trap in the inland wilderness. Douglas achieved a compromise regarding maritime trade: HBC could do so providing it used ships sailing under the Mexican flag with Mexican captains. Alvaredo did, however, permit Douglas to buy cattle and sheep to supplement the livestock at Fort Vancouver — they were from the governor's own herds and he profited mightily.

Monterey, Alta California, February 1, 1841

Dear Mr. Simpson,

As requested, I report a second time to you on the matters of interest in Alta California. Regarding the site of a possible trading post, I recommend Yerba Buena [San Francisco] as the ideal location, which lies on a sheltered shore of a vast tidal basin. I also determined that the company should not consider entering into retail trade here, as first thought, because this requires recruiting and paying a sales force. We should continue with the more familiar wholesale business of supplying goods to merchants in return for hides, tallow, and grain.

I led an investigative expedition inland from Monterey with thirteen company men and two Californians, and enclose the map I drew of our route. The crime rate is high here, and the justice system is inadequate and incompetent. Most women are of doubtful morality. However, the region has immense potential, which under Mexican rule has seen little development.

I remain your obedient servant,
James Douglas

Douglas fell in love with the sunny climate and the countryside and seriously considered living there. The opportunity presented itself to him in the form of cheap land, but in the end he declined the offer. His recent promotion reduced the temptation. Later, when HBC built Yerba Buena's fort, he was too busy with complicated challenges to move.

Douglas came home in March 1841 in time to meet the United States Exploring Expedition, sent out to the Pacific for scientific and survey purposes. Knowing his fascination with geography, McLoughlin assigned Douglas to the leader, a naval lieutenant named Charles Wilkes. Douglas took great pride in showing Wilkes around the fort and the countryside, explaining HBC's operation.

The American had been expecting a community of loose morals and lax behaviour according to his intelligence and was surprised that he found the opposite. The small trade school that the two chief factors had established to train the orphans and offspring of the company's servants impressed him most. Wilkes wrote in his journal: "Douglas appears a shrewd & intelligent gentleman about 40 years of age, tall & good looking with a florid complexion & black hair."[2] He also noticed and praised Douglas's unusual humanitarianism. For his part, Douglas missed his new friend when the expedition sailed away.

Family life was important to Douglas, more so than it was for many men of the period. He never got enough of it and endeavoured to provide his children a better experience than he had. A believer in education for girls as well as boys, Douglas taught his daughters to read and write, and Amelia honed her own literacy skills with them. Following his father's example, Douglas also instructed his children in other subjects such as arithmetic and the natural sciences when time permitted. He planted seeds for them to study how they grew, and when they germinated the plants spelled the girls' names.

Amelia was the singer and storyteller of the family and taught her children the Cree legends in her native tongue. At her knee the girls learned the fine art of sewing and embroidery. Douglas ensured his daughters were fluent in both French and English.

Neither did he neglect their spiritual education. Douglas was well versed in scripture from his Scottish school days and from reading the Bible when he ran out of books. As was the custom, he read the Bible aloud to his family in the evenings and led them in prayer daily. He expected their attendance at the protestant service every Sunday and often joined Amelia and the girls at Catholic Mass held in the fort's chapel. Douglas was neither for nor against either form of Christian expression.

The children had known only Fort Vancouver as a home, and Amelia and James had lived there together longer than anywhere else. They were happy and settled in a comfortable life they expected to go on forever. But as political pressures grew between Britain and the United States and more and more settlers arrived, Douglas reluctantly predicted that the cozy, secure world they loved wouldn't last.

13

Vancouver's Island

A visit from George Simpson, the governor of the Hudson's Bay Company, in August 1841 confirmed for James Douglas that life was changing. In the absence of John McLoughlin, Douglas welcomed his superior with as much pomp and ceremony as he could muster. After Simpson inspected Fort Vancouver, he invited Douglas on a tour of the Columbia Department by sea, going as far north as Sitka.

On a warm summer day, Douglas stood with Simpson on the deck of the SS *Beaver* as it nosed around the southern tip of Vancouver Island. Shading his eyes, he caught glimpses of two big harbours and the land around them. He listened to Simpson describe the need for another fort, which would be HBC's fallback position if the forty-ninth parallel became the boundary.

"This place looks promising," Douglas said. "I want to go ashore."

"Our schedule is too tight," Simpson told him.

So Douglas had to be content with a tantalizing long-distance view of the place he thought might be his future home. The two men returned to the subject many times on the voyage. Although the Americans were lobbying for the forty-ninth parallel, the governor believed Britain had a strong case for the Columbia River and Douglas was convinced of it.

When they returned to Fort Vancouver, Simpson took Douglas aside for a walk. "I'm still anxious about the location of Fort Vancouver. Whichever way the negotiations go, the centre of the Columbia Department will end up either deep in U.S. territory or just across the river from it."

"Too close for comfort on the north bank?" Douglas asked.

"Much too close to the Americans." Simpson pointed across the river. "Wherever the boundary ends up, I've decided to establish a new headquarters on Vancouver's Island, anyway."

"Well, that will certainly strengthen Britain's claim to Vancouver's Island," Douglas said as they strode along the river.

"Another bonus is that supply ships won't have to cross the bar at the mouth of the Columbia. That causes too many delays waiting for calm weather both coming and going, and we lose ships, which results in disastrous shortages and diminished profits." Simpson rested his hand on Douglas's shoulder. "I want you, and only you, to undertake a detailed survey of the potential site. Our plan is of such strategic importance that you must do it next year."

Douglas's heart sank. He was going to have to warn Amelia and the girls. Although he fully supported Simpson's reasons to move the headquarters, he had little enthusiasm for the task.

In the summer of 1842, as Douglas had anticipated, settlers flooded into Oregon Country, which confirmed it was only a matter of time before the boundary question surfaced again. He returned, as ordered, to Vancouver Island to identify a site for the new fort. This time he sailed, not in the *Beaver*, but in the smaller schooner *Cadboro*.

Dressed practically in thick trousers and sturdy leather boots, Douglas shoved a telescope and knife through his belt as he stepped into a small boat from the ship. Sailors rowed him, six HBC employees, and their gear to Clover Point in sunshine. The men climbed a shingle beach and tramped more than a kilometre to one of the two harbours Douglas had seen from the *Beaver* the year before. The open grassy areas, the cooling breeze off the Pacific, the protected anchorage, and views of sea and mountains impressed him. Later he wrote that he had found "a perfect Eden in the midst of the dreary wilderness of the North west coast...."[1]

The survey party avoided the Native villages clustered on the far side of the harbour and didn't meet a single person from the Old World. After several long days of roughing it, Douglas had found not one but four potential sites for a settlement. Among the bays and inlets they discovered land with fertile soil suitable for farming and woodland to provide timber. Douglas was concerned about the limited supply of fresh water but knew that wells, once dug within the fort, should provide enough. With his usual attention to detail he also met and talked with the local Natives who lived on the water's edge. Their numbers and assertiveness made him note that the company might run into difficulties with them when construction started. Douglas contemplated incentives to ensure the Natives' co-operation.

Seated by the campfire, he drew a remarkably accurate map in his notebook, and after weighing the benefits of the possible sites, wrote a report to his superior that recommended one.

Camosack, August 18, 1842

> I had to make several trade-offs to get
> what we want. I chose the site with a protected
> harbour that has deep-water moorage alongside
> a natural rock wharf, so ships don't have to
> unload at anchor. This spot has good, flat land
> to build on but doesn't have the advantage of a
> clear view out to sea.

Douglas had chosen to position the new HBC western
headquarters in what we now know as downtown Victoria.
He called the site Camosack, the local First Nations' name for
"gorge." His name didn't stick. While Douglas was surveying
southern Vancouver Island, HBC passed a resolution that the
new fort must be built without delay.

When the *Beaver* sailed back in mid-March 1843, it carried
Douglas, fifteen HBC labourers, and a Catholic priest. The hold
was crammed with construction equipment, supplies, and trade
goods. Douglas oversaw the unloading of men and materials
in dry weather and immediately ordered six men to dig a well.
Then he set about acquiring timber for the stockade and bastions
that would surround a medium-sized fort. He involved the local
Natives and offered one blanket as an incentive for every forty
pickets. They soon began arriving. Work continued apace with
men squaring timber and the stockade lengthening each day.
The weather co-operated.

Every night, being a keen observer of the heavens, Douglas
watched a light streaking across the clear black sky from dusk
until moonrise obscured it. Carefully, he noted the phenomenon's
appearance in his journal until it ceased, but he was unable

to explain it. What he had seen was the Great Comet of 1843, visible throughout the Pacific Northwest. While Douglas had enough scientific knowledge to understand the comet wasn't an omen, others were more superstitious.

When Douglas was satisfied construction could proceed without him, he sailed north to close the fort at Taku (Juneau) and McLoughlin (Bella Bella). They had proven too costly, and in future the *Beaver* would collect the furs from the trappers. Once done, he brought the men and supplies from those forts back to southern Vancouver Island to augment the workforce there. Now Douglas could sleep in a log hut, one of several completed. He made a thorough inspection of the progress during his absence, and before leaving in early June he left detailed orders for the work he wanted accomplished during the summer and fall. He kept in touch with the chief trader left in charge by letter. By October the stockade and bastions were complete, and at the end of 1843 several substantial buildings were finished. Douglas hoped his work there was complete.

The fort went through several name changes that year before Douglas's superiors at HBC finally decided on one they thought was suitable. Douglas's early choice of Camosack was changed to Albert in honour of Queen Victoria's consort, which was used on the West Coast during the spring of 1843. But HBC reconsidered, and by June the name became Victoria.

14

The End of Fort Vancouver

The summer of 1843 brought changes around Fort Vancouver, too, when 875 Americans from Missouri settled to farm the land. Over the next two years 4,400 more poured in. Despite the population jump and the escalation in the settlers' efforts to gain annexation to the United States, James Douglas still believed the international boundary would be the Columbia River.

During those years, Douglas and Amelia welcomed baby Alice into their growing family, and he began to dream of a long leave in "civilization." His mother had died in British Guiana in 1839 and his father in 1840, so he felt a strong need to pay his respects to both. He requested the leave for 1846, but events intervened in 1845 to dash his hopes.

Douglas shouldered added responsibilities while John McLoughlin mourned his son's murder at Fort Simpson and his son-in-law's suicide. Afterward, McLoughlin lost heart, and

Douglas sadly watched as the man opposed more and more of Governor Simpson's orders, diminishing his worth in the eyes of the company.

The second event that blocked Douglas's journey to Europe and South America was the election of James K. Polk, a new American president. In March 1845, Polk had ridden to power on a platform that promised to claim all the territory south of the fifty-fourth parallel on the West Coast, which included the Alaskan Panhandle and the Peace River district. Alarmed, HBC sent the annual supply ship directly to Fort Victoria and ordered the trade goods at Fort Vancouver moved there, too. Troubled and fatigued, Douglas soldiered on. Territorial battle lines were forming in the Pacific Northwest, and spies were infiltrating.

Fort Vancouver, October 15, 1845

Two British Army officers arrived at Fort Vancouver last August to whom I extended a good welcome. Using their "holiday" as a cover, they toured extensively, made inquiries behind our backs about the settlers' view of the HBC presence, and assessed the fort's defences. Both McLoughlin and I took them at face value. Later we were surprised to learn the officers had delivered a detailed report to HBC authorities in Montreal about the state of affairs in the Columbia basin. In it they described how we were encouraging American settlers by providing supplies and failing to uphold British interests in the region by participating in an unofficial "government."

Who had sent the officers? Simpson? McLoughlin has been trying Simpson's patience recently, so it could have been the governor. I can't find out, but I'm still furious over the officers' deception.

The negative report resulted in the London Committee of the HBC appointing a three-man Board of Management to run the Columbia Department, which diluted McLoughlin's power. He was a member, but Douglas and Peter Ogden, another chief factor, joined him at the wheel. By the end of 1845, McLoughlin was gone.

Fort Vancouver, January 15, 1846

The loss of the McLoughlins was a blow to my family and me. They had lived next door to us for fifteen years, sharing many ups and downs, meals, and social occasions. Amelia was as close to Marguerite as best friends could be. They were each other's support during John's and my long absences, and through the inevitable tragedies of life. I shall miss them a great deal, as I have known John for twenty-seven years and he did so much for me. It is a sad, sad time.

At the end John even offered us half his new property in Oregon City in an attempt to keep us together. But he has decided to become an American, and I have chosen to stay loyal to Britain and HBC despite the turmoil.

> I declined his offer as gracefully as I could.
> We keep in touch with the McLoughlins at least
> for now, and Amelia and our four daughters
> have accepted Marguerite's kind invitation to
> visit in late August.

On her return to Fort Vancouver, Amelia gave birth to another daughter, whom they named after Marguerite.

In June 1846 the signing of the Oregon Treaty settled the boundary dispute but not Douglas's peace of mind. The dividing line between the territories of Britain and the United States became the forty-ninth parallel for all time, putting Fort Vancouver in American territory. At the coast the boundary dipped south through the islands in the Strait of Georgia and then followed the middle of the Strait of Juan de Fuca to the open Pacific, leaving the southern tip of Vancouver Island and Fort Victoria under British control. The mainland north of the forty-ninth retained HBC's name of New Caledonia.

On hearing the news six months later, Douglas characteristically took a solitary walk. His mind raced over the implications, but his heart cracked. As he gazed at the river and then his home, the realization hit him: he was standing on American territory. His years in *la jolie prairie* were over. He had won the struggle once for a life of peace and abundance; now he would have to begin again. No doubt HBC would move him into British territory, if not immediately, then certainly within a couple of years. He didn't want to go. Douglas buttoned his coat against a winter breeze and wondered why he had thought Britain would prevail. His hopes of further promotions seemed slim. He trudged on, wondering how to break the news to Amelia and his daughters. Tired and despondent when he returned to his office, Douglas picked up his pen:

Fort Vancouver, December 10, 1846

> I have just learned of the boundary settlement and the outcome astounds me. Not only that, it is unclear whether the islands between the mainland and Vancouver's Island belong to the United States or us. Surely, they are ours?
>
> Britain has betrayed everything we have worked for — forts, farms, settlements, even our way of life. It's monstrous. I fear my career will stall at best and decline at worst …

Despite his melancholy, Douglas wasn't someone to shirk duty. The boundary decision had created problems for HBC, and he had to solve them quickly. Not the least was the immediate need for a new brigade route within British territory from the north to Fort Langley. The rugged coastal mountains were almost impenetrable by canoe, on horseback, or on foot. Following the Fraser River was the obvious choice, but it was far too treacherous for canoes between Fort Alexandria and Fort Hope. Douglas wondered if packhorses could get through the mountains along the Fraser's banks, so he sent a subordinate to reconnoitre. None of the three attempts to find a safe route was ideal, so in his typical leadership style, Douglas went to see for himself.

August 20, 1847

> The mighty Fraser has lived up to its name. All routes I saw involve building trails on steep to vertical mountainsides, often high above the raging river, and need a fleet of boats to get the

brigades from below the rapids to Fort Langley. One alternative, which reduces the need to negotiate the dangerous paths along the eastern bank, requires crossing the river at Spuzzum using boats to carry the 200 horses across the wild river. The western bank looks safer to me, and there is room to build a resting place lower down the river.

If we can devise a means to get the brigades across Fraser's River, I think this latter route can work. I called the resting place Fort Yale.

Fort Langley personnel broke the trail on the west bank below Spuzzum over the winter, and the brigade of 1848 was the first to test it. The river crossing resulted in heavy losses. The brigades used it in 1849 and then abandoned Douglas's route. After that they followed the Kamloops trail south beside the Okanagan River, turned westward (at Osoyoos) along the Similkameen Valley, wound through the coastal mountains into Hope, and continued by water to Fort Langley and Fort Victoria.

The loss of the Columbia basin hurt HBC in other ways that Douglas had to manage. First, American customs duties now on all supplies delivered to Fort Vancouver reduced profits. Second, the increase in settlers had put pressure on Native territories, resulting in rising hostility on both sides. This resentment escalated into kidnapping and murder in November 1847 when the Cayuse attacked a mission farm in Washington Territory. As soon as Douglas heard the news, he dispatched trade goods from Fort Vancouver to provide the ransom to free forty-seven white captives. He hoped it would prevent an American reprisal against the Cayuse, but his efforts failed. The Cayuse War in

1848 further disrupted trade, farming, and transportation in the region, to say nothing of safety.

The pressures mounted for Douglas — furs declined, trade slipped, and food became scarcer with the interference to the Columbia basin's agriculture. And if that wasn't enough, in May 1848 the HBC's annual supply ship from London foundered on the Columbia bar and lost its entire cargo worth £30,000. On the personal side a nasty influenza epidemic swept the fort. Little Marguerite succumbed, and her grieving parents buried her beside their other four children lost in infancy. Douglas shipped out for the Sandwich Islands (now called the Hawaiian Islands) shortly afterward on a quest for supplies to replace those lost. On his return he had little time to spend with his grieving wife before he left on his semi-annual visit to Fort Langley. Douglas hadn't expected easy years after the boundary decision, but 1848 was the worst.

In the last year of the decade Amelia and Douglas had another baby. He named this daughter Rebecca in memory of his maternal grandmother who had outlived his mother. Douglas's nostalgia for his carefree boyhood in Guiana prompted this choice.

Far away from the Douglas family in the Pacific Northwest, HBC in London was focusing on ramping up its diminishing sphere of influence.

Fort Vancouver, February 2, 1849

The company's petition to the British government to grant it Vancouver Island and the mainland above the forty-ninth parallel will have been decided by now. If they get what they've requested, it may benefit me. I sorely

need some encouragement to maintain what
little hope I have left for my career.

HBC didn't get everything it wanted but did receive
Vancouver Island with certain conditions attached. The royal
grant of January 1849 stated that the company had to establish a
colony and allow settlers to buy land from HBC. Also, it allowed
HBC to keep only 10 percent of the revenue it received from land
sales and other commercial activities related to the settlement.
The rest had to be spent on the growing colony. Britain gave
HBC five years to fulfill the terms or Vancouver Island would
revert to the Crown.

Less than two weeks after Rebecca's birth in March 1849,
Douglas received a letter from the governor of the Hudson's
Bay Company. He opened it eagerly. As he read, he slumped in
his office chair and put his head in his hands. Simpson's letter,
written ahead of the signing of the royal grant, said he was
posting Douglas to Fort Victoria as chief factor and temporary
governor of the proposed new colony because he could be better
spared from Fort Vancouver than anyone else. The unfortunate
phrasing hurt Douglas who believed HBC was sidelining him.
He poured out his resentment in a private letter to Simpson:

Pray, what does the appointment of "Governor
of Vancouver Island *pro tempore* imply? Does it
mean that I am to be thrown aside like a cast-off
garment when the heat and toil of the day is over?
If so, I am not ambitious of such honours ...[1]

But Douglas had overreacted and possibly misinterpreted
the meaning of the letter. As the senior HBC officer on the

West Coast, surely he was better suited to take charge of the new headquarters on Vancouver Island as Fort Vancouver faded into oblivion.

Whatever was meant, he and his family had no choice but to move north. But they didn't go alone; in the end, the entire headquarters staff and all the equipment and supplies accompanied them. The Hudson's Bay Company abandoned Fort Vancouver to the Americans in May 1849.

15

Fort Victoria

If James Douglas was angry about the move north, the prospect of being the new colony's governor did give him something to anticipate. However, Amelia had no such reward awaiting her in the remote and small Fort Victoria. She was leaving five dead children in the wooded cemetery at Fort Vancouver, knowing she would be unlikely to return, and was filled with a worry that tore at her heart. Tiny Rebecca had caught typhus, an often fatal disease.

Once on the trail north, Douglas faced difficulties of his own: a slow-moving wagon train, a bull he had bought en route, and stragglers. The wagons were piled high with what Douglas called "their booty." Furniture, family treasures, more than 272 kilograms in gold, and otter pelts worth £30,000 made a tempting target. He carried his Thompson map in his saddlebag in case the booty was stolen.

The column crept north. Douglas and his three eldest daughters rode on horseback, while Amelia, in the last wagon, tenderly cradled Rebecca in her arms for the entire journey. Then Douglas's prize bull escaped, and despite an energetic search, he never saw the animal again. In low spirits the family boarded the *Cadboro* on June 1 for the last leg to Fort Victoria.

The ship encountered light breezes in Puget Sound, and when the vessel finally anchored on June 6, the family got their first view of their new world. It wasn't reassuring — Fort Victoria appeared small and basic. Once ashore, Amelia looked eagerly for her new home. Plain and utilitarian, it had none of the refinements she was accustomed to or expected. Worse yet, there was no woman to greet and assist her. Douglas had anticipated his family's reaction but could do little to ease their disappointment.

Fort Victoria, August 30, 1849

My family and I remain disenchanted with Fort Victoria. We feel forgotten here, so far is it from trade routes and civilization. We are cut off from affairs and help. If it weren't for the supplies we carried from Fort Vancouver, we would be even more uncomfortable.

I am beset with disgruntled company employees, hostile Natives, *another* complaining chaplain who also serves as schoolteacher, and a severe water shortage.

The summer has been hot. The river that supplies our waterpower at Millstream, which grinds the grain and saws the wood, ran dry, and the drinking water from the well I ordered dug in 1843 proved insufficient. Grass and forest fires threatened the fort and frightened everyone.

The soil layer above the bedrock is thinner than I first thought, and I fear it will not support enough crops for a growing colony. Previously, this outpost relied upon food from the Columbia farms and supplies from Fort Vancouver's stores to supplement its needs, but we must be self-sufficient immediately now that the plentiful source has dried up along with our water.

As an autumn storm assaulted the fort, Douglas sat deep in thought at his small desk, seeking solutions. Instead of workable ideas, his anxiety grew. The fort hadn't been able to supply enough food to the coal miners bound for Nanaimo when they dropped into the fort. The arrival of settlers in the near future would put impossible demands on their hospitality and provisions. Despite being so far from the trade routes, Douglas estimated that ships would call more often now, seeking to top up their water and buy supplies.

He considered the personnel problems, too. That summer a passing ship had brought reports of a gold rush in California, and poorly paid HBC employees deserted to try their luck at a quick fortune, leaving too few to do even essential work. Their replacements had protested the lack of beef for dinner by refusing to work; others stopped because it was raining. Snorting with impatience, he had no time for this sort of attitude. The loss of baby Rebecca, who had never fully recovered from typhus, also intruded into his thoughts.

Then Douglas turned to his recently delivered mail. He began sorting it into two piles — one from HBC and one from the British government. He worked through the former. Suddenly, he let out a cry and jumped to his feet, knocking over his chair. HBC had written to tell him that, due to parliamentary squabbles in London, the company had appointed someone else to be the colony's governor. Once in control again, Douglas read on, his lips tightening.

Richard Blanshard, a young barrister with no experience in North America or with HBC, was the new governor, due to arrive in 1850. Douglas, HBC wrote, was to remain chief factor of New Caledonia and become the company's agent north of the forty-ninth parallel responsible for land sales to colonists. HBC suggested his agent's salary might go as high as £200, but nothing was certain. Douglas clenched his fists, partly because he was passed over and partly because he would lose income.

Fort Victoria, April 30, 1850

On March 9, with a foot [thirty centimetres] of snow on the ground, the thirty-two year-old governor arrived, earlier than expected. I scrambled to provide a seventeen-gun salute for him. Blanshard was discomfited that his official residence was still unfinished — indeed, it was barely begun due to lack of labourers and urgent work that took priority. He had to live onboard HMS *Driver* for a month and expressed his distress to me endlessly. I made him welcome and attended his commissioning ceremony in the mess hall, but with little enthusiasm. He is not the man for the job.

When HMS *Driver* set sail, the governor's house was still not ready, and I provided a room in my home for Blanshard and one for his manservant. The arrangement will last six months, and I don't enjoy his proximity or conversation. Indubitably, when he moves out, he will be displeased with his new accommodation and bitterly complain. After spending more than a quarter-century sleeping on the ground, snowshoeing for miles, suffering frostbite and mosquitoes, I have little sympathy for him. Blanshard seems bewildered that Victoria isn't the reasonable-sized town he had anticipated, but a fort!

HBC explained the difference between governor and agent to me in detail. I am in charge of all the HBC affairs, the fort, land sales, and trade. The governor is in charge of the administration of the civil government of the colony and military affairs. As there is only one settler so far and no military force on the island, Blanshard has little to do. He is resentful of my authority. I try to be respectful and keep my distance from him.

Blanshard believes he is entitled to the discount that HBC employees enjoy at the company store and whines incessantly that he has to pay top prices for his supplies. But it is the lack of a 1,000-acre [405-hectare] estate he had believed was awaiting him and my greater power that irritate him the most. I doubt he has the fortitude to last long here.

Douglas was right — Blanshard tendered his resignation in October 1850 after only eight months. Britain's acceptance took nine months to arrive, and Douglas became acting governor. He wasn't thrilled.

While a disgruntled Blanshard awaited his departure, Douglas ignored him. He had urgent matters to occupy him. For HBC to colonize Vancouver Island in keeping with the royal grant, it had ordered Douglas to acquire large tracts of land that, as agent, he would then sell to settlers. Although the land on the island was the traditional territory of the twenty thousand Natives who lived there, HBC instructed Douglas to obtain every hectare he could, leaving the tribes with land on which they had built their houses or had cultivated. For the rest HBC paid £1 per band member, not per hectare, to keep its expenditures low.

Wearing his HBC hat, Douglas energetically acquired land, using skills gained over many years of trading with Native tribes. He never called these land negotiations treaties, but "purchases." However, treaties they were, and his letters to HBC show he knew the agreements were designed to extinguish aboriginal title. He believed, as everyone did in 1850, that the First Nations could only benefit from the "superior and more civilized" European society and would long to become a part of it. Policy of assimilation was the order of the day, if not yet law. Douglas also wanted the aboriginals gathered into the Christian church. That First Nations people might not have the same opinions simply didn't occur to Douglas or anyone else. He saw himself as a benevolent father who knew best.

Fort Victoria, October 15, 1850

I concentrated on purchasing land around

Fort Victoria first and then went farther afield to Sooke, Nanaimo, and Fort Rupert [Port Hardy]. Around Fort Victoria I negotiated fourteen separate purchases with Native chiefs, costing HBC about £700. I promised the Indians we wouldn't disturb them in their villages, resorts, fishing stations, or while working their fields, but told the chiefs they couldn't sell those areas to anyone else in the future. I also made it clear they were at liberty to hunt and fish as they had always done and would enjoy the same rights as all British subjects.

Whether the chiefs clearly understood the implications of the agreements is uncertain. Did they realize they were losing traditional territory and wouldn't be able to get it back? Did they understand it was "forever"? The chiefs signed with their marks, an *X* probably guided by an HBC hand, on blank pieces of paper that Douglas planned to fill in once he received the proper wording from London. Much got lost in translation — some chiefs thought they were signing peace pacts, others didn't know what they were signing.

Hard though it is to believe, Douglas was fairer and more respectful in his dealings with the aboriginal bands than other people were. As he laid the groundwork for the incoming settlers, he genuinely aimed for peaceful coexistence between the First Nations and the new colony to benefit both. He worked hard to avoid the disaster he had witnessed in 1847 when the surge of settlers took aboriginal land for themselves that triggered murders in Washington Territory and the Cayuse War. Douglas always protected the Natives' right to their village lands and fields, and the right to hunt and fish where they always had. Others who followed were less generous. He also sincerely tried to ensure that the Natives understood they had all the rights and privileges of any British subject, including recourse to British law in the event of disputes. But how much the aboriginal leaders understood about that aspect of their changing fortunes was limited in the extreme.

While he negotiated with the Natives, Douglas also wore his acting governor's hat and fought with HBC on behalf of future settlers. He strongly opposed HBC's land policies, which were driving colonists south of the border where land was free. He urged a free land grant of up to 300 acres (121 hectares) per family to attract more colonists to Vancouver Island. But HBC ignored his suggestion and decreed every settler had to pay £1 per acre (a little less than half a hectare), as well as buy a minimum of twenty.

Then, wearing his keen investor's hat, Douglas took personal advantage of the land for sale that he had acquired for HBC. After worrying if the price was too high, he sold himself property on the shores of James Bay near the fort.[1] Here he built the first private house on Vancouver Island and boasted that it was the biggest and best.

Fort Victoria, August 25, 1851

> My workload is wearing me down, what with the land purchases for HBC and everything else to do with the fort and new colony. I am exceeding overstretched and feel set upon from all sides. To this effect, I hinted to Simpson that I have had enough of it all.

But to no avail. A few days ago a letter arrived appointing me as Blanshard's permanent replacement. When first offered, I would have quite liked to have become governor despite believing Simpson was removing me from affairs. Now that I have been doing the job, I am far from certain I want it.

16

Governor at Last

James Douglas's fatigue and frustrations were at the root of his lack of enthusiasm for his new appointment. Now forty-eight, with grumbling employees, wayward settlers, and a family still suffering homesickness for Fort Vancouver, he wanted some peace and comfort strongly laced with praise. Worst of all, he faced growing opposition from within to his elevation to governor.

British settlers had been dribbling onto Vancouver Island through Victoria since the Douglas family had taken up residence in the fort. The colonists weren't all hardy, adventurous types. Those more used to the comforts and refinement of town life expressed shock at what they found. Others expressed anger that the best land around the fort was unavailable — HBC and its staff having acquired it all. The settlers who planned to farm had no option but to look elsewhere for ideal spots to homestead. The land on offer was expensive, and though Douglas had been lobbying HBC for this to change, the new settlers thought the prices were his fault. Their other irritant was the one that had irked Richard Blanshard — they had to pay exorbitant prices for food and supplies from the company store. As the fur trade drew to a close, HBC discovered there was a good profit in the colonization business.

Fourteen disenchanted settlers had coalesced into Douglas's opposition. When Douglas was chosen to replace Blanshard, they penned their discontent to the outgoing governor. Their major anxiety concerned Douglas's conflict of interest between the business affairs of HBC and the best interests of the colonists. The disaffected settlers couldn't imagine that Douglas would be impartial when it came to decision-making or the resolution of disputes. Their letter demanded the immediate formation of a Legislative Council to dilute Douglas's power.

In fact, the British had instructed Blanshard to appoint a council before he even set sail for Fort Victoria. He had been unable to comply initially because there weren't enough landowning colonists who were independent of HBC to participate. In his waning days in power the departing governor had appointed a council of three — true they were all landowners, but two were Douglas and a retiree from HBC. So despite every objection, HBC still held the balance of power. James Cooper, the only settler on the council, was one of the dissenting colonists. The council met for the first time on August 30, 1851, a few days before Blanshard sailed home.

From then on Douglas performed a delicate balancing act — maintaining profitability of the company as the fur trade dried up and administrating the independent settlers who soon outnumbered HBC personnel. He also had the responsibility of providing for the physical, mental, and spiritual well-being of the entire colony in a more democratic society than he had ever experienced in his life. None of it came easily to him.

Douglas had spent his first two decades in the wilderness without the comforts and amenities that towns and cities offered. He had spent the past decade as a leader with almost absolute power and was unfamiliar with opposition. He was used to being obeyed without question and to imposing disciplinary measures when he wasn't. Could he adapt? Did he want to?

Fort Victoria, September 2, 1851

Although I had expressed serious misgivings about accepting the permanent governorship, when the commission arrived, I began to consider it with more interest. The commission itself is an impressive parchment scroll from which a massive red wax seal dangles on a red ribbon. It reads: "Governor, Commander-in-Chief, and Vice-Admiral of Vancouver Island and its dependencies ..."

I have decided to accept the appointment unreservedly, to stay and make it work. My letter of acceptance to the British government expresses how very honoured I am. I told them my goals for the colony after considering the responsibilities and duties, priorities and budgets, the appointment implies. One of my main objectives is to improve the conditions in which the aboriginals live, which I consider deplorable. Others include the abolition of slavery among the Native tribes and the establishment of the church of Christ here on the edge of the Pacific.

Happy to have decided on his course of action, Douglas sold himself more property and preserved the area between his two lots as a park for the colony.[1] Douglas also offered lots to HBC's senior staff ahead of the settlers, enabling them to acquire many hectares of prime land on southern Vancouver Island. In doing so Douglas had ignored his opposition's warnings about conflict of interest and the likelihood he would favour HBC's interests over the settlers.

Douglas breathed a sigh of relief to see his family settle down as social life and amenities expanded. Now Amelia had women friends, all but a couple of mixed blood and similar experience, and she became the first lady of a tight society. The children were growing up. Cecilia, the eldest, was fifteen now and helping her father with clerical work; the younger ones attended the fort's small school run by the chaplain. And Amelia was pregnant again. Douglas yearned for a son and heir and spent a few blissful moments every day dreaming how he would raise a boy worthy of following him.

With his elevation in rank, Douglas assumed an air of *gravitas*. The unkind called it pomposity, and Governor Simpson wrote that Douglas was becoming "imperious." The governor was certainly reserved and outwardly unemotional, which led to accusations of coldness. Both his leadership position and his natural tendencies led to this impression. In public he seldom smiled, found small talk an effort, and displayed a singular lack of humour. His distant demeanour rarely thawed except within the confines of the family home. His clothes were much mended and outmoded, and the more fashionable settlers thought him "provincial."

Although Douglas was a man who hid his feelings, he was faithful to his wife and was a devoted family man who adored children. He had been regularly sending money to his Guyanese sister, also called Cecilia. When her daughter, another Cecilia, went to an expensive school in Germany, Douglas willingly paid the fees, and at the end of her education, subsidized her passage to Victoria for a visit. He never revealed why he invited her, but a need to reconnect with far-flung family was clearly surfacing as he aged.

The Douglases, eager to meet Cecilia, were at Esquimalt early. When Cecilia walked down the gangplank, it was the first time his wife and children had met anyone from his side of the family. Douglas immediately noted her pale skin and then her stylishness. Cecilia was a refined young lady, and Victoria was an unlikely destination for her. She was astonished by its lack of sophistication, but to her credit she accepted it. Cecilia stepped in to provide clerical help to her uncle as his own Cecilia became ill. She assisted Amelia during and after her aunt's confinement and set a fine example of manners and deportment for her country cousins.

Amelia gave birth to the Douglases' only son who survived to adulthood in June 1851, a few weeks after Cecilia arrived. With fatherly pride and high expectations, Douglas named their twelfth child James William, after himself and his father-in-law. But James Junior was a sickly boy whom Amelia spoiled rotten, and his health and lack of intelligence caused his parents anxiety throughout his childhood. Their daughter, Cecilia, had also been a source of concern that year — she had nearly died of an unknown complaint despite the tender care of John Helmcken, a young doctor newly arrived from England.

Amelia had grown short-tempered while adjusting to Fort Victoria, and she began to tighten the reins on her daughters as they grew up. When she realized Helmcken was falling for Cecilia, she gruffly discouraged his attentions. But the doctor persisted, and blessed with an optimistic outlook on life, eventually won over Douglas. Amelia took longer.

Fort Victoria, July 21, 1851

As Cecilia is ten years John Helmcken's junior and still only fifteen, I worry she is too young for marriage. I have told them both that I will not give my consent until I have made some inquiries into John's suitability. They are aware it will take many months to receive answers from England. I want proof that Dr. Helmcken is both single and properly qualified.

Once Douglas heard that Helmcken was all he said he was, he willingly gave his approval to the happy couple. However, Amelia remained sharply unenthusiastic about the union. When Douglas wheedled the reason out of her, he bought a small parcel of land close to theirs for the couple. Amelia couldn't bear the thought of Cecilia leaving her.

Although Douglas struggled to operate in the best interests of HBC and the settlers, he was progressing in one area — infrastructure — but not in the matter of defence.

Fort Victoria, September 1, 1851

For some time now I have been taking stock, seeking solutions, anticipating the needs of a growing colony. This has allowed me to identify some needs of both the company and the colony that are mutual and urgent — roads, schools, and churches.

I petitioned HBC in London for funds and personnel to build roads and bridges to link the more distant homesteads to the fort and the sea. A surveyor is to come out. As the children of our poorer settlers and company labourers are at risk of illiteracy, I have asked the company for money to open two protestant schools, one for Esquimalt and another for Victoria, to teach the basics. This money, if it is forthcoming, will provide the necessary schoolrooms, furniture, and salaries. The school, already operating in the fort, serves the boys and girls of HBC officers and provides a more in-depth education. Another serves Catholic children.

As governor, I requested that the British Colonial Office encourage the missionary societies in Britain to send out protestant clergy and missionaries to minister to the settlers and convert the Natives. This is a desperate need here.

As commander-in-chief of the colony, I am concerned with our lack of defences. I told Britain the infant colony is vulnerable in case a Native uprising takes place as it did in Washington Territory. We are impossibly outnumbered. I am also aware the Americans might push north …

In fact, Douglas had some evidence to support his latter belief. After rumours circulated about gold on the Queen Charlotte Islands, American ships began stopping at Victoria on their way north carrying prospectors. As these islands and the mainland weren't under the governor's control, Douglas couldn't prevent American incursions into this part of British territory. However, Britain was apathetic, and without permission, Douglas acted. He appropriated the HBC vessel *Recovery* and ordered its crew to take possession of the only surface gold seam in the Charlottes for the Crown. Later Britain appointed Douglas lieutenant governor of the Charlottes.

This action demonstrated Douglas's characteristic willingness to take command decisions on his own and to report what he had done afterward. Such behaviour revealed audacity, perhaps arrogance, as well as foresight. It also spoke volumes for the position he was in both as governor and geographically. As responses from his superiors took nearly a year to arrive, he had to resolve urgent problems himself. Although he had the Legislative Council to consult, he wasn't used to doing so and made decisions alone. This lack of consultation didn't endear him to the council or to the colonists. But despite their criticism Douglas continued to act unilaterally as governor. This tendency earned him a reputation as a dictator. In such a remote outpost of the empire west of the Rocky Mountains, with his background and personality, that was inevitable.

Douglas enjoyed promoting the new colony and turned out to be a vigorous sales representative. He encouraged the British government to recruit settlers from not only Britain but also California, which had joined the United States in 1850. He also recognized the advantages of attracting small businesses such as sawmills to Vancouver Island. As he swung into his stride as governor, Douglas wrote frequent, persuasive letters to correspondents spanning the globe. He began to make things happen, and his enthusiasm rose to new heights. Nothing was too small or too big to interest him. His energy was boundless.

17

Consolidating the Foothold

In 1852, James Douglas congratulated himself as his projects
got underway and reported progress in letters and reports, as
well as in his journal:

Fort Victoria, October 7, 1852

One of my proposed schools has opened
in Esquimalt and is teaching eighteen boys.
Parents provide the school supplies and pay
£1 per year per student, which supplements
the teacher's salary; HBC has provided the
schoolroom, the teacher, and his board
and lodging. As I am a strong supporter of
education for girls, I am assisting a colonist
to open a girls' school and have told HBC to

give the recommended teacher free passage to Victoria.

Survey work on the proposed roads has progressed, and some clearing has been achieved on the routes to Metchosin and Sooke. I doubt that carriages will be able to use the roads, which aren't much more than rutted tracks, but they are adequate to handle livestock, pedestrians, and hopefully horse-drawn carts.

The farms of the Puget Sound Agricultural Company are flourishing in our temperate climate and now provide much food for the colony — meat, milk, butter and cheese, grain for flour, and fruit. My early worry of not being self-sufficient is over, but the farms need to become profitable. Timber is increasing revenues since HBC began exporting it to California.

I have recently inspected the coal mines near Nanaimo. What I found is very exciting indeed — new seams have been discovered. Minerals mean money, and increased production will turn a tidy profit for the company. (And that means my annual share goes up, too.) A ready market for coal exists in California, and as more shipping lines convert to steam, money should pour in. I asked HBC to send twenty qualified miners to better exploit the opportunity. In preparation for the expected surge in Nanaimo's population, I also decided it was time for an elementary school to open and transferred a teacher from Victoria to start it.

> This is all most gratifying because the coal
> trade will likely set Vancouver Island on the
> world map at long last.

Douglas had permitted John Helmcken and Cecilia to plan their wedding for Easter 1853, but in November 1852 an unfortunate incident took place that resulted in bringing the date forward. Douglas was breakfasting when he heard that a murder had occurred near the fort — the first. The victim was a shepherd, one of two who worked the HBC flocks. His companion found his body in their home with two gunshot wounds in the chest.

Abandoning his meal, Douglas rushed to the crime scene. His examination found personal property missing, including four guns, and evidence scattered around that included a Native pipe. He suspected two aboriginal youths, one of whom HBC had fired from the sheep farm.

Douglas, following HBC's policy of speedy punishment, immediately dispatched messengers to the chiefs of the tribes from which the suspects came and demanded they surrender the two youths to him. He offered a reward but didn't expect results. He was right. The Cowichan tribe was the most uncooperative Douglas had encountered while acquiring land to sell on Vancouver Island. It had refused all his efforts to negotiate.

For justice to be seen to be done, Douglas planned an expedition to Cowichan, which he predicted would be dangerous. Since he wasn't getting any younger, he was apprehensive for the first time in his life about his safety. He couldn't delegate his role, but if anything happened to him his family would lose its provider. He saw Helmcken, if the man was already a son-in-law, as the answer. Without consultation Douglas brought his daughter's wedding forward to December 27, 1852.

Snow blanketed the fort as staff finished preparing the mess hall for the ceremony. Douglas kissed his beloved daughter on both cheeks at the doorway and stood proudly as Cecilia took his arm. Solemnly, he guided her between the rows of chairs to John's side. As Douglas joined his wife, he noticed Amelia's strained face.

Afterward, everyone accompanied the bride and groom back to the family home amid a ripple of musket fire, booming of cannons, and the pealing of the fort's bell. The HBC personnel in the mess hall received grog (rum) and a feast to mark the occasion. Helmcken recalled that the private party, too, was a scene of revelry and joy.

After the reception was over, John and Cecilia spent their honeymoon in their temporary home — Blanshard's old residence. They kept to themselves for several days, and when they finally reappeared, Amelia harshly scolded the newlyweds and accused them of neglecting her. John and Cecilia graciously forgave her, putting her tantrum down to worry over her husband's imminent departure to locate the murder suspects.

As Douglas anticipated, the Native bands didn't surrender anyone, though he had given them a month to respond. On January 4, Douglas led a heavily armed posse out of the fort to dispense justice that he hoped would be a deterrent to anyone else considering committing crimes against the colony. The *Beaver* and the *Recovery*, carrying Douglas's force and large numbers of Royal Naval personnel, steamed north up Vancouver Island. The ships anchored off the mouth of the Cowichan River.

SS *Beaver*, January 5, 1853

Once ashore, I ordered a tent pitched and
a beacon lit on a nearby hill, then summoned

the Cowichan. I dispersed my eleven French-Canadian guards around the perimeter of the meeting place and waited alone in the tent. My pistols and cutlass were close to hand, and many valuable gifts were displayed for the band to see. Soon war canoes swept up to our ships filled with two hundred yelling warriors ready to attack, outnumbering my force.

When the chief and elders trooped into the tent, I rose to my feet and demanded in a loud voice that they give up the murderer or else I would burn their lodges and annihilate their tribe. (I have always found going on the offensive makes the best start in these situations.) After a long parley and my promise of gifts, the chief produced a man. I suspect he was a slave substitute, but knew it was all I would achieve.

I duly arrested him and sent him under guard to the *Beaver.* I then addressed the assembled Natives about their future relationship with the colony. The nerve-wracking event ended with no bloodshed.

The posse headed to Nanaimo where the second suspect had fled. This time they had difficulty finding him, and it wasn't until January 16 that they finally arrested the culprit hiding in the forest. The same day Douglas convened a court on the *Beaver* and tried the pair by jury, the first assembled in the colony. Both suspects confessed to the crime, and the non-Native jury quickly found them guilty. Governor Douglas sentenced the two aboriginal men to hang by the neck until dead. He had had the foresight to bring along a hangman, and the sentence was carried out in front of the entire tribe on Protection Island at a place now known as Gallows Point.

At Sea, January 18, 1853

I dispensed justice with the full force of British law. I sincerely believe the sentence was the only way to secure peace and prosperity for both sides of the incident. The risks were considerable, both to my person and to British rule here. My life was spared thanks to my daring, which Natives always admire, my knowledge of aboriginal behaviour, and my personal guard. Whether this episode will subdue these bands sufficiently remains to be seen.

There were no more murders, but Douglas didn't gain co-operation from the Natives afterward, either. The Cowichan resisted settlers on their land for another decade and never signed a treaty, despite continuing attempts and offers of money and goods.

As more and more British men and women settled on southern Vancouver Island, the Douglases began to feel a racial prejudice they had only experienced once before from the missionaries visiting Fort Vancouver. Amelia's efforts to keep Cecilia close might have been a reaction to the sting of this first overt discrimination in Fort Victoria from purebred British settlers who could be unbearably superior. Amelia's lack of fluency in English didn't help. Douglas didn't fare much better, but his language skills and position insulated him more. Amelia, though wounded by the intolerance, remained active. She hosted outings for the fort's children, and as "first lady," provided a welcome and hospitality for all female newcomers. She even nursed some when they fell ill and acted as midwife to a few. Gradually, those with a mixed-race background became a minority.

Fort Victoria had expanded during its first decade, with eighty-seven buildings inside and outside the fort itself. In 1853, Douglas added another HBC member to the Legislative Council and appointed four magistrates for the colony. Still lacking a church, he ordered a Protestant one built in 1853, but it took three years to finish. However, the Catholic Church had a strong presence even before Douglas moved to Victoria permanently. Demers, the gentle Roman Catholic priest who had baptized Douglas's daughter, Jane, had arrived in 1847, already a bishop.

Fort Victoria enjoyed tax-free status for its first few years, but this enviable state didn't last. As more and more people arrived and alcohol was cheap, the inevitable happened. Public drunkenness increased and became the catalyst for Victoria's first tax.

As governor, Douglas always sought ways to fund the growing colony, and because he deplored those who over-imbibed, he thought the opportunity to impose a levy to solve both problems was too great to miss. He decided to tax alcoholic beverages at both the wholesale and retail level. The first time he presented his idea to the council, James Yates, who owned a saloon, objected fiercely. The second time Douglas succeeded using deception. He called a last-minute council meeting when Yates was away. Reluctantly, the browbeaten council members voted to implement liquor licences, and Yates never forgave the governor. Within a few months Douglas was able to report less drunkenness and more money for day-to-day operating expenses.

18

Ruler, Not Politician

James Douglas became increasingly unpopular as Victoria expanded. The colonists saw his tactics to overcome opposition as unsympathetic, usually unilateral, and certainly undemocratic. His long isolation in the fur trade and immersion in the dictatorial ways of the Hudson's Bay Company had insulated him from the more progressive ways of Europe and eastern North America. Furthermore, when stressed and opposed, Douglas became more domineering, failing to listen to others or remember to build consensus. But Douglas knew no other way to conduct himself or business. He was a ruler, not a politician.

Soon word of his high-handedness reached London for the second time. Several senior HBC officers and the disaffected council member, James Yates, signed statements requesting that the British government appoint an independent governor and institute an elected house of assembly. Douglas was bewildered when he found out and unable to understand why these leading residents were so critical of him.

One reason that prompted the letter of opposition involved the San Juan Islands. Douglas still smarted over the boundary settlement and coveted all the islands scattered between Vancouver Island and the mainland, insisting that the British-American border settlement had left the islands' ownership uncertain.[1] He told the British government in 1851 that he intended to assert British sovereignty over all the islands. The next year he ejected some Americans "squatting" on one island. In late 1853 he sent an armed party to take possession of Lopez Island. His justification and fear stemmed from his belief that if the Americans got the San Juans, they would seal off the maritime trade route and ruin the colony's commercial enterprises. Douglas's reports resulted in HBC, not Britain, claiming San Juan Island on which there had been a company fishing station since 1850, and HBC reinforced that claim by establishing a large farm that prospered. The Americans held their peace for the moment.

Douglas also made the mistake of giving the best jobs to family members. Never a good idea wherever it was done, it was a dreadful idea in the tiny society of a new colony. His niece's mother and husband from Guiana joined the Douglases in the summer of 1853. They had come to live, not visit. Douglas hadn't seen his sister, Cecilia, since she was born the year he sailed for Scotland with his father forty-one years earlier.

Sister Cecilia's husband was David Cameron, a former manager of a sugar plantation in Guiana who had run into financial difficulties. Governor Simpson had offered him a job as head of personnel in the Nanaimo coal-mining operation, which Douglas had probably arranged, though Cameron denied it. But it was Douglas's appointment of Cameron as the first judge of the new Supreme Court of Vancouver Island that caused uproar in the colony. The man had no legal experience whatsoever.

The tumult lasted more than a year, and seventy-one colonists and HBC staff signed yet another petition for the colonial secretary, which pointed out that the close family connection would lead to prejudiced justice. Ringleaders included members of the Legislative Council and the chaplain, who was the subject of the new chief justice's first case. He had been accused of stealing pigs, and though he was acquitted, he felt shoddily treated ever afterward. James Yates, the saloonkeeper who had unsuccessfully opposed liquor taxes, hosted the group's meetings in his Ship Inn, which Douglas viewed as bordering on mutiny.

Douglas and the Protestant clergyman Robert Staines had always butted heads over the lack of democracy in the new colony. Douglas couldn't grasp the chaplain's idealistic view and believed the man was fomenting dissent in the colony, especially with newcomers. He was also exasperated with Staines's inability to understand HBC's authority. For their part, Staines and many others believed Douglas had grown arrogant since his appointment as governor.

The petitioners decided Staines should carry their document to England and deliver it in person to the British government. It never got there — Staines drowned when his ship sank in a storm. A second copy of the petition did reach London, but not until Douglas's own letter had preceded it, reporting how prosperous Victoria was growing and justifying the appointment of his brother-in-law as the most fitting person available. Douglas won this battle — both the government and HBC supported Cameron's selection. With Staines no longer able to make trouble in the colony, Douglas was now certain that dissent would end. However, he hadn't reckoned with the press.

Fort Victoria, January 6, 1855

I have continued to suffer strain as events at home and on the world stage began to push on Fort Victoria. I have had to manage threats from Native tribes, all of which I averted using my skills with the Indians. The nastiest involved the Tsimshian and Tlingit from the Alaska Panhandle, who arrived here bent on avenging a murder of one of their own at Fort Nisqually. I was infuriated when an American official had the temerity to accuse me of encouraging them to attack as I had actually expended considerable effort on their behalf trying to persuade the Natives otherwise.

The war between Britain and Russia has made me fear for the colony's safety.[2] I believe the Russians, near in Alaska, could come south to invade the closest British territory within thousands of miles. I have energetically taken steps to defend the colony. I regret that the Royal Navy never accepted my earlier offer to maintain a naval storage facility at Esquimalt as that would have ensured their greater presence on our Pacific Northwest coast. I have sent entreaties to the British government for naval ships and heavy guns to defend the fort.

There is a great necessity for a military force raised from colonists and the local tribes to go north to attack the Russians. Astonishingly, the rest of the Legislative Council didn't support this proposal, and they defeated my careful plans. Instead, they chose to station a force of thirty (!) men on the SS *Otter* to protect the colony against marauding Russians. Then the British government informed me it could send an occasional naval vessel to look in at Fort Victoria, and little else.

But unknown to Douglas, Britain was actively negotiating with the Russians to protect the foothold of British territory on the Pacific.

19

Moving Toward Democracy

During these years of tension, daughter Cecilia had her first baby, a boy, making Douglas and Amelia proud grandparents for the first time. Their joy was short — his parents found him dead in his crib one snowy January morning. The family sadly buried the baby in the Helmckens' garden. Amelia, pregnant at the time with her thirteenth and last child, was especially affected.

Six months after their grandchild's funeral Amelia delivered Martha, who the couple named after Douglas's mother. A month later Douglas sent his wife and baby, and the Helmckens, away for a long holiday at Fort Nisqually. Douglas wanted to keep his family safe from the threat of Russian invasion. He hoped that Cecilia would find a change helpful as she grieved, and he needed a breather from his wife's growing negativity. During the visit, Cecilia conceived again, and this daughter, named Amy after Amelia, survived.

Douglas took many long walks and solitary horseback rides in these unstable years as he constantly sought ways to improve the fort's lack of preparedness. Alone he devised many schemes to protect the colony from frequent threats.

Fort Victoria, September 16, 1855

The Native bands grow bolder, perhaps because of rapidly encroaching colonization. I have recently handled an invasion of a sort — two thousand warriors from northern nations arrived on southern Vancouver Island earlier this summer. I never discovered what their true motivation was in coming here.

As I have no means of containing any outbreak of violence should it occur, I tolerated the Native presence in the settlements because I dare not reveal the colony's weak defences. It was a calculated gamble to take with only a tiny militia. I then took the sole action remaining, and one I have always favoured over force: I demanded a parlay with the chiefs. I clearly told them if their people remained friendly and well behaved, they could work for the settlements to earn money and trade goods. As usual my offer of an incentive worked like magic, and at the end of the summer, the Natives peacefully returned from whence they had come considerably better off. But I know that such successful outcomes might not always be that easy to achieve.

Concerned about my family's safety with so many unknowns related to the northern Native presence, I again sent Amelia and my two youngest children to Nisqually. My daughter, Cecilia, with our three-month-old granddaughter, accompanied my wife, and they were away for four months. I dearly missed the youngsters.

When the family returned, the Russian threat had evaporated after the finalized agreement between Russia and Britain to respect each other's neutrality on the Pacific coast. Douglas rejoiced on both counts.

However, all wasn't well in the American territory where Amelia and Cecilia had been holidaying. Just after they left Nisqually, Natives had attacked American settlements around Puget Sound, as well as east of the Cascade Mountains, with tragic results. Douglas assisted the Americans in Washington Territory by sending supplies and ammunition to them, bought with his own money, but otherwise stayed out of the conflict. He viewed the Americans' preference for armed might rather than negotiation with the aboriginal peoples as the wrong approach to the problem. His method of maintaining good communications with Native people and using incentives were paying dividends in the British colony. The governor was lucky in one respect — the Natives on Vancouver Island disliked and distrusted one another more than they desired to fight the colonists. Douglas capitalized on this mutual enmity between the tribes throughout his governorship, and the strategy served to keep the British settlements safe. Most settlers on Vancouver Island supported Douglas's more peaceable approach.

Although the local threat from Russia had vanished, Douglas was still occupied with his wish to turn Esquimalt into a naval base. When the British admiral in command of the Pacific Station in Chile wrote asking for support for his fleet fighting the Russians in the western Pacific, Douglas jumped at the opportunity. Without authority from London and with no idea if the Royal Navy would pay for it, the governor ordered tons of coal from Nanaimo for the ships, built a naval hospital, asked Fort Nisqually for two thousand sheep and cattle, and got his colonists to grow vegetables for the fleet's impending arrival. The ships did come and Douglas did meet the admiral, but the hospital only treated one casualty, a man with scurvy, not war wounds. That said, Douglas had moved his dream of a naval base a step closer, and it would soon stimulate the economy and social life of Victoria.

Fort Victoria, June 2, 1855

A new clergyman sailed into the harbour of Esquimalt last April 1. Edward Cridge and his wife responded to the call for a replacement after Robert Staines drowned at sea. The Cridges are made of sterner stuff than their predecessors, uncomplaining and keen.

This new HBC chaplain, who is also a qualified schoolteacher, is just the person I envisaged ministering to the colony. He appears robust and energetic, and lacking in all prejudice. He is a person I anticipate will have a profound effect during his five-year contract period. He favours a plain worship that appeals much to me, since I grew up attending the Scottish kirk.

As chief factor, I supplied Cridge with land and a house and promised him the Victoria District Church when finished. I will appoint him the colony's first inspector of schools next year. I believe he and I will get along handsomely, given our similar philosophy on life and faith.

By the mid-1850s, Fort Victoria had overflowed the fort's palisade and was home to 232 residents out of the 774 colonists on Vancouver Island. Half were under twenty years old and none was over sixty. The number of inhabitants grew steadily each year, and private homes and businesses sprung up outside the fort. The farms produced abundant harvests, both in quantity and variety, though the farms were costly to run. The small militia expanded and drilled regularly.

Fort Victoria, December 15, 1855

I am happy to say my personal finances are healthy. My two substantial salaries and HBC's annual profit-sharing income, which has risen sharply, netted me nearly £1,500 in 1854 alone. However, my outgoing expenses rose proportionally, and I had to spend a fair amount of my earnings. I kept buying land, had built and furnished my James Bay house, and clothed my increasingly fashion-conscious daughters. They have begun ordering expensive dresses from London. Amelia now wears black silk, and I bought two of the regulation dress uniforms for chief factors.

Being an avid reader, I encourage my offspring to take after me, and so we order many books every year. I am reading *The Practical Astronomer* and *The Decline and Fall of the Roman Empire* at the moment. My niece, Cecilia, petitioned me for a piano, and I managed to find one for sale by a departing settler. She is now teaching her cousins to play. I also have to buy large quantities of sheet music from San Francisco and London to maintain their accomplishment. We are becoming quite refined.

At last social life was thriving in Victoria. Everyone participated in card parties, picnic outings, riding, and even canoe trips farther afield. The younger residents organized dances, soirees, and parties as they kept one another occupied and got to know newcomers.

Douglas had always enjoyed the nightly dinner for HBC personnel in the mess hall. He had continued this tradition at

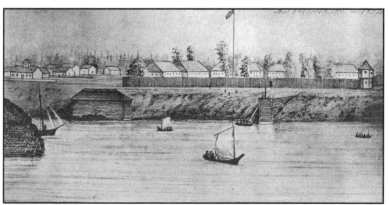

Fort Victoria, 1854, five years after the ground was broken.

Fort Victoria with considerable ceremony and presided at the table of senior officers every night. Occasionally, outsiders attended, and these invitations were a coveted ticket among the more affluent colonists. Dinner was formal, with tables laid with white linen, silver cutlery, and sparkling crystal. Douglas made his entrance after everyone had gathered and said grace before the first of three courses was served. Men enjoyed soup, meat or salmon, and a dessert, accompanied by wine. After the toast to the queen was proposed and drunk, the junior officers withdrew, leaving their superiors to enjoy a pipe of tobacco and conversation. Douglas never allowed frivolous chat during or after the meal — he came primed with a topic to get the diners talking, sometimes political and sometimes scientific.

As gentlemen's clubs did in Victorian London, the mess dinners exerted a huge influence on the day-to-day affairs of the colony. Men concluded business transactions as they puffed on their pipes. They also avidly debated global and local politics. Before there was an elected body representing the colonists, the diners often reached decisions on their behalf. But that was about to change — abruptly.

The uproar over Douglas's appointment of his brother-in-law as judge compelled the Colonial Office in February 1856 to order Douglas to call an election of people's representatives to an assembly that would govern Vancouver Island. Douglas was far from enthusiastic. He wrote back complaining that the effort of arranging it dismayed him, and he should await proper legal minds to arrive to advise such a body. His delaying tactics failed, but his strict guidelines for suitable candidates and voters succeeded.

As a man of his time, the governor not only fiercely opposed women having the vote but also restricted the upcoming ballot to men who owned more than twenty acres of land. He justified this measure by explaining that only such landowners would have the intelligence to vote in the best interests of the settlers. Those wishing to run for office also had to be male but had to own more than £300 worth of property. This narrowed the field to only nine eligible men. Only the District of Victoria fielded enough candidates to hold a campaign; the rest were elected without a contest.

The colony's first election on July 22, 1856, produced seven representatives — three for Victoria, two for Esquimalt-Metchosin, and one each for Sooke and Nanaimo. A small assembly, to be sure, but it was a move toward a more democratic ideal that had been slow in coming. John Helmcken, Douglas's son-in-law, was a member for Esquimalt-Metchosin and became the assembly's first speaker.

On August 12, 1856, the swearing in of the first Legislative Assembly of the colony took place in the company mess hall. A homemade table for the speaker stood at one end, with six chairs for the new members arranged in a half-circle before it. Benches for the audience lay behind the members' seats.

Governor Douglas addressed the gathering with great solemnity. He recapped the difficulties and progress of the past five years and then detailed reasons for optimism in the future. He made those listening very aware of their new responsibilities: "The interests of thousands yet unborn may be affected by our decisions...."[1]

The assembly changed the name for the most southerly settlement on Vancouver Island to Victoria. A year later an unprecedented event taxed Douglas and the members to their limits. It also put the insignificant colony permanently on the world map.

20

The Fraser River Gold Rush

After dinner one night in the mess hall, men sat transfixed as James Douglas emptied a few shiny yellow grains onto the white tablecloth. It was gold from the mainland. A few weeks later he produced a large bottle that was half full of placer gold that Natives had collected from the sandbars of the North Thompson River. Jaws dropped. It was spring 1857.

Victoria, May 1, 1857

I had first heard of gold on the mainland in 1855, or perhaps earlier, when the Natives began trading small amounts to HBC outposts in the interior. I also knew about the mini-gold rush of 1854 in American territory east of the Cascade Mountains that ended abruptly when the Indian war broke out. Some of these prospectors had pushed north into our British territory and discovered where the Natives had found gold. I had hoped not much would come of it given the greed and chaos of the California rush in 1849.

But now that large amounts of the precious mineral were in my hands, I realized we are likely to be overrun. I lost no time in informing the British government of its implications to our far-flung colony. I explained gold's tremendous significance and what had occurred in San Francisco when its discovery caused the population to explode from one hundred thousand to four hundred thousand in a matter of weeks. We are woefully unprepared in Victoria if word filters out about the Fraser River's abundance. It is only a matter of time, I believe.

The Natives found the placer gold while grubbing around in the sand and gravel bars on the Fraser River above and below the canyon. They told a HBC trader that there was a lot more. I didn't doubt it as I hefted the bottle in my hands last night. The aboriginals appreciate what they have discovered, and believing the gold is theirs, are resisting, sometimes violently, the few intrepid Americans who have made their way north. Trouble is brewing and may well erupt in the spring of 1858 if hordes of veteran miners from California descend on the riverbanks.

But Douglas, as governor, had no jurisdiction on the mainland, just on Vancouver Island. As chief factor of both regions, all he could do was maintain the exclusive rights of HBC to trade with the Native bands around the Fraser River. Frustrated by Britain's sluggish response to his requests for assistance, Douglas kicked into high gear as 1857 drew to a close. He took action without the authority of HBC or Britain, and illegally as it happened, but hoped for future forgiveness.

In late December 1857, Douglas, as the closest Crown representative and the senior officer of HBC on the mainland, declared that Britain owned all gold found in the Fraser and Thompson rivers and their tributaries and prohibited anyone to mine it without permission of the British government. He not only informed all the HBC trading posts on the mainland, but he also chose to have his proclamation printed in newspapers in Washington and Oregon. It was another of his typically bold strokes and one that the Colonial Office decided to support, even praise, after the fact.

Whether his actions would suffice, Douglas had no idea, but he knew he had to do something to control the expected invasion. Evidence suggests that the newspaper insertions did the opposite, but it was the exaggeration in American and British newspapers of the first assay results that ignited the fire. The first three hundred men to react to gold's temptation abandoned their jobs in March 1858 in Bellingham's coal mines and Vancouver Island's sawmills to sail directly to Fort Hope. The race was on!

A year almost to the day that Douglas had first impressed the diners in the mess with gold dust, the first prospectors hell-bent for the gold fields sailed into Victoria harbour. The extended Douglas family, dressed in their Sunday best, had just stepped from the Victoria District Church and stood in astonishment as gold-hungry men disembarked from a dilapidated ship. The boisterous crowd, four hundred all told from San Francisco, scrambled ashore with picks and shovels swinging from their shoulders, and firearms and knives shoved into their belts. They wore slouch hats over long, unkempt hair and were none too clean.

Other worshippers pressed the governor for information. He was evasive, trying not to alarm the Victorians. The first boatload outnumbered the residents in one go, and Douglas knew his time had run out. He told everyone to go home and walked over to the prospectors to deliver a speech of welcome and warning.

Day after day, more and more people with gold fever made their way to Victoria, initially from Washington, Oregon, and California. They had left employers with no staff, families without providers, and ships without crews. Later others came from farther away — the East Coast and even Europe. Hopeful prospectors poured up the Fraser River in any craft that would float. The price of skiffs and canoes in Victoria inflated to the point that miners couldn't afford them. Instead, they banged together crude rafts for the two- or three-day voyage that, likely as not, didn't survive the passage. Others bribed Natives to paddle them. Within ten days Douglas estimated that more than a thousand miners had roared through, leaving Victorians gasping.

This gold-driven invasion of Victoria followed closely on a U.S. Supreme Court decision that had ruled no black persons, even those who were free, could become U.S. citizens. The judgment had horrified the part-black Douglas.

Among the passengers on the ship that the Victorians had watched so intently after church were thirty-five American blacks who had come to Victoria at Douglas's invitation. After hearing of the miserable discrimination they were enduring in California, Douglas had instantly moved to help them.

Victoria, April 30, 1858

I met three members of the "Pioneer Committee" the day after they arrived and, we all agreed, had excellent discussions. I am pleased to find they are God-fearing Christians. They held a joyful service of thanksgiving in a rented room the night they came. Sadly, others didn't view this as I did and complained about the noise of their energetic worship.

I promised the blacks freedom and equality here: they could buy land and start businesses immediately. They were delighted they would be able to vote within nine months of settling on their land [Douglas was incorrect] and would be protected by British law from the start. After seven years, I told them they could become British subjects. The blacks could hardly believe their ears and shook my hand right heartily.

Reverend Cridge met them the day after I did, and the blacks gladly accepted his invitation to worship at his church. He tells me they have no wish to start their own churches or in any way separate themselves from the community. Cridge was impressed to discover that several plan to earn enough money to free their relatives from slavery and bring them to Victoria. His enthusiasm for the immigration scheme delights me. I saw it as yet another reason to celebrate his appointment.

Some of the first thirty-five blacks bought land in Victoria, a group started a company making bricks, others secured employment on the farms, and one opened the first store in competition with HBC.[1] Word of the opportunities in the colony flew back to California, and boatloads of black immigrants began arriving. In all about eight hundred sought refuge and a new life in Victoria, determined to integrate with the colonists. Several homesteaded on Salt Spring Island.

However, Douglas and Cridge were in the minority when it came to welcoming the blacks. American colonists, especially, were aghast. But Douglas stood firm against them and the intolerance. Of course, his motivations for doing so ran deep: his own origins and those of his wife certainly played a part in relating to the blacks' plight; his humanitarianism, stemming from his strong Christian faith, generated an attitude of inclusion unusual for the era; and his drive to populate the colony also influenced his invitation.

Few colonists or HBC staff knew where Douglas had been born, but some guessed and many wondered. He had never been open about his roots with his company colleagues, but within the family he was speaking freely for the first time. The arrival of his sister, with whom he spent many evenings hearing news of Guiana, meant secrets evaporated as his entire family learned about his origins. Now the Douglas children, Amelia, and other relatives spent time discussing their differences in skin colour and appearance. They eagerly watched new babies to see how they would look as they grew. Would they have fair or dark skin? Would the hair be blond or black, straight or curly? Whom would the baby resemble? And Douglas was the one who most enjoyed the speculation.

The influx of gold seekers transformed Victoria overnight, and residents had difficulty adapting to the change. The

Amelia Douglas in the mid-1850s

settlement of God-fearing, polite inhabitants lost its family feel of a small community and became a place filled with strangers. The Victorians faced an onslaught of mostly young and unattached men, some of whom were hard-drinking and disorderly and all of whom were desperate to get their share of the wealth at any cost. A tent city sprang up reminiscent of a medieval army camp. Prejudice resurfaced from European residents, most of which was directed toward the miners and blacks but spilled onto those of mixed race; disdain for a colony viewed as backward became widespread; and personal safety was jeopardized. Amelia withdrew to avoid a racial intolerance made worse by her halting English, but Douglas relied on his position to protect him from discrimination.

Victoria, May 20, 1858

On one hand, I relish the high profits HBC earns selling supplies to the miners for their outfits, but on the other I worry we will be unable to control them, provide for their safety in a harsh wilderness most are unprepared for, or protect them from the hostile Natives. Most nominally American, the gold-crazed men have little respect for British law in the territory in which I have no jurisdiction. I briefly thought I could prohibit them from the area altogether but quickly realized that would be impossible to enforce. I also fear the loss of British territory on the mainland, recalling the annexation of Oregon Territory to the United States following the demands of American settlers.

In 1858, before the British government fully understood the risks inherent in the gold rush in their territory on the Pacific Ocean, Douglas had issued another proclamation. Wearing his HBC hat for the mainland, he announced the requirement of licences for ships in British waters. If the vessels didn't have a licence, obtainable only in Victoria, HBC would seize and destroy them along with their cargo. This edict had no more authority in law than his first, but it served to control vessel traffic, count heads, and force the prospectors through Victoria to buy supplies at the company store.

As the invasion swelled, Douglas sent another plea for naval reinforcements to London and the Royal Navy's admiral in charge of the Pacific Station. Then he set sail to inspect the "diggings" near Fort Hope for himself, not forgetting to take his Thompson map.

SS *Otter*, June 23, 1858

> I found gold in abundance, much more than I had anticipated. One group of prospectors was hauling in fifty dollars' worth each day and those farther upstream were doing even better.
>
> I also faced the fallout of the first confrontation between the Indians and the miners. The local aboriginals, armed to the teeth, had threatened to remove the miners by force if they continued to pan for gold. I will be reporting this to London and suggesting it is likely the first armed attack of many, given my expectation of one hundred thousand miners. Unless something is done, and soon, lives will be lost.

> After considerable reflection during this visit, I discarded my earlier approach based on the mainland being the preserve of HBC and moved to the position that the whole area must be placed under civil government. Bearing this in mind, I plan to collect $5 licences from every miner and require compensation for any infringement of HBC trading rights. Anticipating Britain will agree, I appointed revenue officers, justices of the peace, and police officers. I also chose several Native magistrates to deal with unruly individuals of their own race in the hopes of keeping the peace at the diggings.
>
> Once home, I will appropriate all the Royal Navy vessels in Esquimalt to control the access to the Fraser River and will man the HBC vessel *Recovery* with naval personnel to assist them.

None of Douglas's actions were legal, but the last did control access to the Fraser River. Douglas hadn't been wrong in his predictions. By mid-July 1858, more than 10,500 excited miners, many of whom were forty-niners, had ventured up the Fraser. The cost of a passage from San Francisco to Victoria skyrocketed, and tickets sold out the moment they were advertised.

In August, but unknown to the beleaguered Douglas, the British Colonial Office acted. An election had ousted the ponderous Lord Palmerston government, and the new colonial secretary viewed the Pacific Northwest important enough to secure the mainland for Britain. With unusual speed the British established New Caledonia as a Crown Colony and appointed

Douglas as its governor. He had got what he wanted — civil government — and *he* was in charge.

The Colony of British Columbia officially came into being on August 2, 1858, and initially excluded the Cassiar and Peace River districts in the north but included the Queen Charlotte Islands. Originally called the Colony of New Caledonia, then changed to Columbia after HBC's later designation for the region, the new entity had "British" added to its name by Queen Victoria when she signed the proclamation.

Douglas didn't learn for another two months of his second governorship. Nor did he know that it came with a condition. He found out both in early October 1858.

21

Governor Again

James Douglas worked relentlessly during the summer and early fall of 1858 before he heard the momentous news. He was in his element, firing on all cylinders as he took command. He chartered two steamers to supply the miners with food and started building a road to reach the junction of the Fraser and Thompson rivers. He welcomed the British Boundary Commission to resolve the precise path of the U.S.-British border through the islands in the southern Strait of Georgia. And he met the Royal Engineers who were to open up the new colony and found New Westminster.

The prospectors, anxious to push farther upriver in search of richer deposits of gold, discovered that the mighty Fraser was impassable as it roared through its narrow canyon above Fort Yale. Their attempts to negotiate it ended in repeated tragedy. Wiser miners followed the old brigade route from American territory into the Okanagan Valley to Kamloops and down the Thompson to the gold fields of the Upper Fraser. Douglas opposed this solution as it shifted the starting point of the gold rush into the United States and out of his territory. Victoria also stood to lose the huge revenue he was banking on to pay for the gold rush, so he proposed a cunning plan to the miners themselves with his usual built-in incentives.

Victoria, September 15, 1858

During the runoff that submerged the gold-bearing gravel bars, the prospectors were unable to work, as I had anticipated. Many were penniless and often starving as game was scarce. I came up with a scheme to assist them and end the loss of life of those who tried to get up the Fraser Canyon. I asked them to build a road around the rapids for nothing but food and my promise they could stake their claims in the richer deposits two weeks before anyone else. Five hundred hungry miners jumped at my offer and commenced work. I expect completion of the 108-mile [174-kilometre] road, as well as the necessary bridges, next month.

My Douglas Trail will begin at the head of Harrison Lake at Port Douglas and follow Anderson Lake and Seton Lake to Lillooet where it will rejoin the Fraser. This road will serve the miners as they spread northward out of the coastal rain forest into the drier Thompson region.

In late October the road was finished, and Douglas cherished all the praise he received for it. One letter pleased him most: it was from the new colonial secretary who had facilitated the road.

However, before this success, Douglas had received severe rebukes from the Colonial Office over his high-handed actions and proclamations while responding to the first flood of miners. Britain told him he couldn't and mustn't use his powers as governor to serve the interests of the Hudson's Bay Company. His regulations were illegal and had to stop forthwith. London revoked HBC's licence on the mainland, due to expire in a year.

However harsh these reprimands sounded, Douglas's Colonial Office superiors weren't about to fire him. Besides, Governor Simpson of HBC had assured them he was the best man for the job. London was simply demonstrating that he could no longer serve two masters — Britain and the Hudson's Bay Company. When the letter arrived appointing him governor of the Colony of British Columbia with a salary of £1,000, it contained the condition that he must sever all connections with HBC. Douglas didn't hesitate. He promised to withdraw immediately from HBC and the Puget Sound Agricultural Company and vowed he would sell his stock. In fact, Douglas did nothing of the kind, hanging on as chief factor for another six months after his commissioning ceremony.

Victoria, meantime, had more tents than houses. Here in a tent city the gold seekers lived while they awaited a means to get up the Fraser. Entrepreneurs who accompanied them grew wealthy by providing grubstakes, whisky, and accommodations. The original merchants of Victoria benefited hugely, too. Gradually, the tents turned into wooden shacks, then into houses. Larger wooden buildings were transformed into brick stores, saloons, and hotels. Land speculation reached a crescendo —

one chronicler reported that three lots bought for US$300 sold three hours later for $20,300.[1]

Occasionally, riots broke out among the miners, and Douglas, against opposition, recruited four black immigrants for Victoria's first police force. Law and order continued to be fragile in the tent city. At the end of July, when some miners threatened to take over the town, Douglas ordered a warship from Esquimalt to subdue them. The Legislative Assembly pressed for a jail, a hospital, and a fire department. Roads pushed north into Saanich, and regular hourly transport ran between Victoria and Esquimalt, the main port of disembarkation.

Victoria, November 1, 1858

All this and more wasn't without cost. I am nearly sinking under the pressure and volume of work. I have none in HBC capable enough to whom I can delegate tasks.[2] In some ways I enjoy the challenge. Fortuitously, none of the dangers I feared this summer and fall came to pass. Whether I was lucky or it was good management doesn't matter — we overcame the struggle.

The new imperial government continues to shower the Colony of British Columbia with assistance. I have received word from London that they are sending a corps of Royal Engineers to the mainland to select a site and lay out a capital city and seaport, as well as construct roads and bridges.

The Royal Navy came through — the eighty-four-gun *Ganges* dropped anchor in Esquimalt in October, the first of several warships diverted north to the newest acquisition of the empire. Not only are the ship and her Marines at my disposal should I need them, but the *Ganges*'s band plays every evening, delighting everyone within earshot, and her officers began hosting dances for the residents. From now on the Royal Navy will maintain a greater presence in the Pacific Northwest. This is the beginning of the naval base I want.

Soon more help was on the way. The Church of England was recruiting an Anglican bishop to oversee the spiritual health of all inhabitants of the mainland and Vancouver Island, Native and non-Native. The governor was pleased about this development, but Reverend Cridge was of two minds. The first chief justice for British Columbia stepped off a ship in November. Matthew Baillie Begbie turned out to be as gregarious as Douglas was aloof. A linguist, an all-round athlete, and Cambridge-educated, he became Douglas's adviser. Begbie carried with him the commissioning scroll that officially named Douglas governor, commander-in-chief, and vice-admiral of the Colony of British Columbia.

The miners, at least those who were well equipped and waited out the freshet, also did well in 1858. Some made $8 a day and others $30. The experienced miners said little about their finds and carried their gold out of British Columbia sewn into their pockets and the lining of their clothes, trusting no one.

In one crazy year Douglas's long-held dream of putting the remote British territory on the world map was now a reality. The gold rush had been the catalyst — for both Douglas and

Britain — to secure the land west of the Rockies and north of the forty-ninth parallel from the expansionist United States.

HMS *Satellite*, November 20, 1858

With a full heart I sailed to my second commissioning ceremony at Fort Langley. My companions included the admiral from HMS *Ganges* and the chief justices of the Colony of Vancouver Island and the Colony of British Columbia.

We spent a comfortable night ashore at Point Roberts and voyaged up the Fraser the next morning. November 19 was cold when we landed at Fort Langley for a welcome by quite a crowd. We trudged up the muddy slope in drenching rain to an eighteen-gun salute from the SS *Beaver*.

The mess hall in the main building was barely big enough to hold us all. The group of men who gathered around me as witnesses to the swearing in represented the Royal Navy, the Royal Engineers, the Hudson's Bay Company, and Native bands. Before Begbie could swear me in, I had to swear him in. Then, with great solemnity, Begbie made me the new governor of the Colony of British Columbia in the name of Queen Victoria. He said I looked very grave while he did so, not at all delighted.

Three important proclamations followed. I announced them all — first, the one that actually

James Douglas, governor of Vancouver Island and the Crown Colonies of Vancouver Island and British Columbia, 1851–1864.

Courtesy Library and Archives Canada C-003316.

declared the mainland colony was under my "rule"; the second that protected all those who had acted irregularly or illegally previous to the formation of the new colony; the third, and the most important, that instituted English Common Law.

At a formal mess dinner that night after the toast to the queen, the honoured guests toasted me with their best wishes. The loyal toast held more significance than usual as I am now Queen Victoria's representative in, not one, but two jurisdictions at the outermost edge of her empire.

This morning after a ceremonious farewell on the jetty, we left to an ear-splitting seventeen-gun salute from the fort's battlements. As the echoes ricocheted around the mountains across the river, all agreed it was a fitting send-off for the new governor.

22

Two Colonies, Nearly Two Wars

Despite the establishment of the Colony of British Columbia, James Douglas still feared annexation by the United States because the American miners were strongly anti-British and outnumbered the colonists fifty to one. Suffering through the hard winter in the shantytowns along the Fraser, the Americans weren't about to give up their gold to Britain. Douglas anticipated conflict. Worsening the situation were grudges held between miners at Yale and Hill's Bar that flared into violence.

Led by Ned McGowan, an outlaw from the United States, the Hill's Bar miners were rednecks to the core and actively subverting British authority. Douglas, having already had one run-in with McGowan, deeply distrusted him. After incidents increased between the factions and the local magistrates, Douglas received overblown warnings about impending mayhem. In January 1859 he ordered Colonel Moody with twenty-five Royal

Engineers, a shipload of Marines, and Chief Justice Begbie to sort it all out.

When ice trapped the ship carrying Moody and Begbie, the chief factor of Fort Langley offered to reconnoitre for them. Moody planned the best strategy on the intelligence he brought back. The colonel left his troops at Fort Hope, and he and Begbie hiked to Yale, meeting with miners along the way so as not to raise the alarm. Once at Yale, Begbie soon determined what was amiss.

However, plans changed when Begbie witnessed a fight between McGowan and Max Fifer, who was the leader of the opposing faction and chair of Yale's town council. The brawl ignited an uproar and sowed seeds for violence in Yale. Moody immediately called in his reserve force, which made a dangerous passage up the river overnight in intense cold.

At Hill's Bar a sentry heard their footfalls across the river at dawn. The force, moving among trees, met a fusillade of bullets from McGowan's rabble army. As ordered, the soldiers and Marines held their fire, knowing retaliation was exactly what McGowan wanted to provoke an international incident or even war. Fortunately, the American gunfire went wild, some said deliberately, and the British contingent marched on unharmed to Fort Yale. The British refusal to strike back defused the escalating conflict.

Begbie was able to hear the charges and counter-charges between the factions and fined McGowan for the assault on Fifer but discharged him of other accusations. In gratitude McGowan entertained the chief justice at Hill's Bar next day with a feast and toasted him with champagne. Douglas fired the magistrates, whom he had appointed, and bewailed the expense of the expedition. But it had been a close call.

Douglas, comfortable in Victoria, still had to make good his promise to withdraw from HBC. But he didn't do it; he clung on and on. His reluctance stemmed from his difficulty breaking a habit of forty years with HBC that was as much a part of him as his skin, and perhaps losing the power he so enjoyed. But by not doing what he had pledged to do he made life frustrating for many, including Alexander G. Dallas, a new son-in-law.

Dallas, a stockholder in HBC and temporarily in Victoria on company business, married Douglas's daughter, Jane, after a two-week courtship just before the gold rush. He was forty and sophisticated, and Jane was eighteen. Since Dallas had no intention of settling close to his father-in-law, whom he considered inadequate, he planned to return with Jane to Europe in May. The gold rush derailed the couple's wishes and more besides.

In July 1858, Dallas had harshly criticized Douglas in a report to HBC's governor. Dallas had written that Douglas was refusing to permit anyone to act as chief factor while he was consumed by the gold rush. Douglas's new son-in-law had also accused the governor of using HBC funds for colonial purposes and vice versa. HBC, already aware a new colony was in the offing and that Douglas would be governor of it, responded by asking Dallas to accept the presidency of the HBC's Western Council. This effectively made him Douglas's replacement. Dallas cheerfully accepted and decided to tell his father-in-law after he withdrew from HBC.

But Douglas still lingered. And the longer he delayed his departure the more he heightened the difficult position facing his business-savvy son-in-law. Dallas, living with Douglas and Amelia at the time, didn't wish to upset family harmony, but as tensions worsened he resorted to avoidance. Weeks lengthened into months, and Dallas never did find a good moment to tell his father-in-law he was to replace him.

In fact, Douglas had had no intention of withdrawing from HBC until the end of May 1859 when the British grant of Vancouver Island to HBC expired. The Hudson's Bay Company finally forced the issue, though. In March it ordered Dallas to present his commission to Douglas and take over. A letter for Douglas accompanied the orders. Dallas held his breath as Douglas opened the letter and read its contents. In the end, Douglas behaved graciously toward his son-in-law, but it was hard for him to do. He surrendered control but delayed informing HBC until early May.

Douglas's foot-dragging cost him his stellar reputation with HBC at the end of his career. His son-in-law's critical report convinced the company that Douglas had failed to serve HBC's best interests during the opening months of the gold rush and had been feathering his nest and those of others for too long. When Douglas tried to secure his HBC pension and a payment from Britain for his time as lieutenant governor of the Queen Charlotte Islands, both were denied. The old fur trader grieved the loss of money and his position and fell back on his dictatorial method of governing.

In the spring of 1859, Douglas added empire building to his repertoire. He dreamed of offices for the treasury, the land office and other government departments, and a barracks built across the harbour from the fort and next door to his own home. He envisioned, too, imposing buildings for the Legislative Assembly and Supreme Court. His extravagant idea of a connecting bridge from the fort to the buildings was the final straw for the elected assembly, which vigorously opposed the whole idea because of the tax burden it represented. Douglas cajoled and tweaked all that stood in his path and eventually succeeded. The bridge at least was built.

The summer of 1859 also saw Douglas fixated once more on the San Juan Islands, which he considered British. The 1846 boundary settlement hadn't indicated which channel among the islands in the Strait of Georgia was the dividing line between British and U.S. territory. Douglas, still harbouring a grudge over the decision thirteen years earlier, claimed it was Rosario Strait to the east of most of the San Juan Islands; the United States maintained it was Haro Strait, closest to Vancouver Island. In fact, Britain and the United States had a joint occupancy agreement in the San Juans, and HBC ran successful operations on San Juan Island itself amid American settlers.

In June a minor incident with a pig gave Douglas the opening he craved, and overreactions brought both sides close to war. An American settler shot a hog from a HBC farm when it was rooting around his garden on San Juan Island, and HBC threatened to evict all Americans from the island if it wasn't compensated. By July an anti-British U.S. Army officer had landed sixty-four soldiers to protect American citizens. They made camp provocatively close to HBC's dock. Douglas reacted by ordering the Royal Navy to use force to remove the Americans from British soil and to begin fortifying the island.

As he often did, Douglas had acted alone, with little or no consultation with the Legislative Assembly. He was so confident this body would support him that he didn't call an assembly meeting for four days while he doled out orders and wrote intimidating letters to the Americans. When the assembly did meet, senior naval officers joined its members at the table, since Rear-Admiral Robert Baynes was at sea. Douglas sat in shocked silence as his advisers recommended withdrawal of all British subjects from the island, the opposite of his bold invasion plan. He strongly disagreed with their view that a confrontation could spark a nasty international incident, a war, or an invasion of Vancouver Island. Douglas's only supporters were the black former American immigrants who immediately established the colony's first regiment, the Victoria Pioneer Rifle Corps, to defend Victoria. The governor supplied their rifles and uniforms.

Although the assembly prevented Douglas's armed intervention, his hard line never wavered and he tried other routes to get what he wanted. He issued a proclamation, claiming ownership of the islands for Britain, and ordered the captain of the thirty-one-gun HMS *Tribune* to take San Juan Island. The captain stalled for time by composing a report outlining the risks and slowly gathering his forces until Baynes returned.

Baynes took one look at the standoff and promptly ordered the *Tribune* to remain alongside. The ship's captain obeyed his admiral and not the governor. But Douglas still kept trying to invade, pestering Baynes to accept his view. By late August, the American camp on San Juan had swelled to 461 soldiers and the island was defended by 22 naval guns. The British rear-admiral refused to have anything to do with the governor's schemes, saying that going to war over a pig was ridiculous. Douglas then gave up and did nothing.

The governor endured persistent questioning in the Legislative Assembly from both sides of the raging debate over what he *did* intend to do, along with unflattering press commentary. In the end, the British and American governments intervened, declaring a joint military occupation of the islands. The Americans reduced their forces, and the British peacefully landed theirs in 1860. In 1872, after Douglas retired, the international boundary became Haro Strait and the San Juan Islands became American. Still believing he was right, Douglas expressed much disappointment over the loss.

Douglas also earned criticism by favouring the Colony of Vancouver Island over British Columbia. Douglas had never intended to move to the latter, but many commented that he should visit more often. But the action that most infuriated those developing the mainland was his decision to locate the colonial offices for British Columbia in Victoria. London finally had to order Douglas to move them to New Westminster, but he delayed carrying out the directive.

Despite Douglas's willingness to lead in a crisis, however misguidedly, he was less adept at dealing with others also in authority. At the outset he had the talented commander of the Royal Engineers in British Columbia in his sights. Colonel Richard Moody was in the unfortunate position of having two bosses — Britain and Douglas. His mandate, in addition to defence, was to open up the wilderness of the mainland with roads and bridges, find an appropriate site for the capital of the new colony, and lay out a seaport. Douglas demanded that the capital should be Derby close to Fort Langley, forty-five kilometres up the Fraser River. Moody disagreed, citing its distance from the sea and its proximity to American forces across the border. He recommended a site nearer the Strait of Georgia, which he dubbed Queenborough. Douglas not only disapproved of the site, but he disliked the name. He wanted to add an *s* and call it Queensborough. Queen Victoria had to referee the standoff. She decreed that *her* new capital would be where Moody selected and would henceforth be known as New Westminster. Douglas and Moody never recovered from their bad start.

In 1860, Douglas declared Victoria a free port with no customs duties. Goods arriving at New Westminster were charged, causing the city to languish. Victoria, of course, thrived to the envy of New Westminster. To appease the residents, Douglas allowed New

Westminster to incorporate and elect a municipal council but said it was too early for the Legislative Assembly they had requested.

Then Alexander Dallas and Douglas locked horns again — as HBC's representative and as governor respectively. This time it concerned land on Vancouver Island. When the royal grant expired in 1859, Douglas claimed land for the British government that Dallas argued belonged to HBC, and the latter launched a lawsuit to prove it. Douglas stopped speaking to his son-in-law, and their mutual antagonism delayed a resolution to the territorial dispute for seven years. Jane and Dallas moved out of the Douglas family house, and their new home quickly usurped the governor's as Victoria's social centre, not only for many of the wealthy residents but also for the younger Douglases.

Then, with Douglas's nose out of joint, Dallas pushed it into the mud. At the time he undertook the lawsuit he was offered HBC's top job to replace George Simpson who had died. Dallas speedily accepted it — it was his ticket out — and he and Jane left for England never to return.

Douglas laboured under the misconception that his position would automatically bring respect and admiration but, of course, it didn't. Public figures tend to attract more criticism than praise, and it was no different in the 1860s. Newspapers opened their offices in Victoria and New Westminster during the gold rush and began publishing editorial analyses of the governor's actions and character. Some were venomous and others held him up to ridicule, but as 1859 progressed and the San Juan debacle entered the mix, the attacks worsened.

Amor De Cosmos, the fiery owner of the *Daily British Colonist* in Victoria, was a loud advocate for democracy and frequently told his readers that the governor was unsuitable and incompetent. Douglas was deeply offended and upset by this abuse when he felt entitled to admiration. He tried to rid himself of De Cosmos by proclaiming a little-known British law that required newspapers to post a bond of £800 in order to publish. Douglas figured De Cosmos couldn't pay it, but he hadn't reckoned with the Victorians who rallied to the newspaperman's defence and the freedom of the press. They raised the bond quickly. When the next edition of De Cosmos's paper appeared, the whole affair made Douglas appear foolish.

As a means of increasing regard for his position as governor, Douglas started to wear a military-style uniform with striped trousers, brass buttons, and epaulettes. He also employed an orderly to accompany him everywhere he went. This servant was not only uniformed but also armed. These efforts failed to increase his popularity in either colony and, indeed, were often the butt of jokes and derision.

Douglas, who had been a sparkling star in HBC's firmament for many years, shone less brightly as a government administrator. He found the shift from dictatorship to democracy difficult to embrace. From the age of nearly sixteen he had lived in the remotest parts of the British Empire, completely cut off from nations where democracy flourished. He hadn't visited Montreal or Quebec City as an adult, had never returned to Scotland, or ever been to London. As far as recent arrivals to Victoria were concerned, Douglas had no idea how modern cultures and administrations operated.

The militaristic character and domineering ways of the Hudson's Bay Company were deeply ingrained in Douglas. Undoubtedly, they had been successful in the early years of the fur trade and exploration, but they served no longer. Douglas had wielded absolute power when he reached the higher ranks of the company and had never seen democracy in action. He gave orders that others didn't question. Douglas was either unable or unwilling to build consensus — he was no listener. Instead, he acted, and usually alone. He had never needed to consult or ask permission in his life and didn't readily learn the skills. This lifetime of power and control made him outstanding as a pioneer and project manager, but a poor champion of representative government.

The changing demographics and social scene had also caught Douglas unaware. As new colonists arrived from Europe, Britain mostly, they were more modern than he was. They certainly had quite different expectations of civil government, society, behaviour, and class distinction. The Victorian moral rectitude and way of life puzzled Douglas, who was used to life in a trading fort that was less oppressive. The newcomers disapproved of mixed marriages; they scorned the leading families' lack of sophistication; they demanded a voice in the affairs of the colony; and they thought nothing of questioning and disagreeing with their governor. Although wealthy, the Douglas family's social standing slipped.

Also, Douglas never figured out why people accused him of favouritism toward his family and HBC. It is hard to say what blinded him — perhaps he believed that giving prestigious jobs to family members was his right, just as he thought he was entitled to automatic respect. Maybe it was his lack of exposure to more modern administrations. With his brother-in-law as the chief justice, one son-in-law as the speaker in the Legislative Assembly, and the other as president of HBC's Western Council, the optics were terrible and undermined his authority further.

When Douglas became a governor, all he could do to gain respect among changing attitudes he couldn't comprehend was to fall back on the pomp and ceremony he enjoyed.

23

The Colony of British Columbia

Once Queen Victoria had settled the squabble over the capital of the Colony of British Columbia, Colonel Richard Moody set his men to work to clear the land for New Westminster. He was profoundly impressed with the natural beauty at the mouth of the Fraser River — the background of spectacular mountains and the rich marshlands of the estuary, as well as the towering evergreens.

Moody did agree with James Douglas in one respect: he was determined to keep this magnificent territory British. Consequently, every task he undertook contributed to that end and, indirectly, to Douglas's vision, whether it was infrastructure or defence. Funds and workers were in short supply to construct the roads, but Moody pressed on undeterred. His engineers felled massive trees on the steep slopes that would become New Westminster and built a customs house and a few shacks for accommodation. It was a beginning. Next came the church.

Douglas sent B.C. Chief Justice Begbie "on circuit" to hold courts at Langley, Hope, Yale, and Lytton, an important way of demonstrating to Natives and non-Natives alike that British Columbia was now under English Common Law. The wilderness of the interior and the hazards it presented to travel never fazed Begbie, despite occasionally proceeding on his hands and knees high above the raging Fraser. The hardy judge was a passionate traveller. He carried his own equipment and supplies and was skilled at living off the land. Begbie paddled a canoe in white water as well as any Native and was witty company around a campfire.

On his first journey on the mainland, Begbie met many aboriginal peoples, and though he wrote that they weren't hard-working, he did comment on their natural intelligence, honesty, and good manners. Like Douglas, he held the minority opinion. But what struck Begbie most was the lack of British settlers in British Columbia — more were desperately needed.

Begbie was as compulsive a journal writer as Douglas, and he shared his notes with the governor for guidance. The notes about his first journey to the mainland made five main points, including the urgent need for safe roads. Without transport of supplies and goods in and out of interior settlements, no farmers could settle and start raising livestock and growing crops. Douglas listened, probably for the first time in his life, because transportation was a subject close to his heart. He bore Begbie's suggestions in mind as he steered the infant colony along.

Not all the governor tackled had negative results. Douglas reduced the price of land by 50 percent in both colonies to attract settlers, and if they had to borrow the money to buy land, he gave them two years to pay it back. He cut the miners' licence fee and established an office to register claims and settle disputes. He ordered improvements to the Douglas Trail to the upper Fraser by which weekly mule trains of a hundred animals supplied the miners. Douglas proudly reported that exports of gold rose to £14,000 each month, and five thousand non-Natives were now working in the Fraser watershed. He encouraged agriculture to support the interior population and planned schools for the Fraser Valley below Fort Hope. Douglas had requested more clergy for both colonies and eagerly awaited the first Anglican bishop.

On his walks Douglas spent hours imagining the future. When the Royal Engineers assessed the old route from the Okanagan Valley to Hope, he ordered them to carve a road through the Similkameen Valley and the coastal mountains. He pondered the implications when miners who had sought gold on the Queen Charlotte Islands pushed their way inland from the coast. They canoed up the Skeena River, explored the Babine Lake region, and reached Fort St. James where Douglas had worked as a young man. Always excited by exploration, Douglas predicted that the Skeena would become an important trade route to the Pacific. Time proved him correct — Prince Rupert later developed at its mouth.

Douglas foresaw the future importance of Burrard Inlet, the huge saltwater inlet that Vancouver and its suburbs now surround. He had the Royal Engineers cut a road from New Westminster straight north to Burrard Inlet. The road opened in 1860, more as a trail, but it did afford early access to the inlet and provided the catalyst for Port Moody. This town at the eastern end of Burrard Inlet became, for a while, the western terminus of the transcontinental Canadian railway.

The governor set his sights on improving the routes to the interior of the mainland and imposed a levy on all goods leaving New Westminster to pay for road construction, later persuading

Hope and Yale to charge similar tolls. His obsession with roads led to the building of the Cariboo Trail of 1863 after Fraser gold was exhausted and miners moved north to the Quesnel River, seeking richer, untapped deposits.

But Douglas's most ambitious dream, originating during his fur trade years, was to link the east and west of the continent by road through British territory. At his end of the vast land mass he pushed bit by bit toward that goal.

Douglas had never neglected spiritual growth in his domains and didn't stop now. He had successfully enticed Christian clergy to settle the Pacific coast and now turned to providing them with churches. Douglas offered almost half a hectare of land to new parishes on which to build. The settlements of Yale, Hope, Derby (near Fort Langley), Port Douglas, and New Westminster were the first to benefit.

When the new Anglican bishop opposed Douglas's generosity, he surprised the governor. What Douglas had forgotten, or had never realized, was that he was now representing the state and not HBC, which had had the right to select and pay clergy. The Right Reverend George Hills, modern in outlook and fresh off the boat from London, didn't want his churches, or any church for that matter, sponsored by or indebted to the state. When, in his usual fashion, Douglas took another run at the issue by offering forty hectares to rural denominations where there were enough worshippers to build a church, Bishop Hills became exasperated. He was angry on two counts: first, because the governor once again had exerted the power of the state on the church; and, second, because Douglas deliberately failed to inform him until after making the offers to the infant parishes. Amor De Cosmos publicly backed the bishop in his newspaper. On the following Sunday,

Hills preached on the dangers of churches accepting gifts of money or land from the state. Expressionless, the governor listened in the front pew.

In the end, the bishop's firm refusals ensured that the colonial government built no more churches for any denomination from 1861 onward. The Anglican diocese, like other denominations, relied on funds from British Bible societies and local subscriptions to buy land and construct its churches in the two colonies. Parishes established around that date still minister to their communities.

The West Coast communication links were improving. A ship sailed regularly between New Westminster and Victoria, and for passengers heading to other Fraser River communities, a sternwheeler ran to Fort Hope. These also carried the mail, a necessity for quality of life for any settler tucked away in remoter regions. The year of 1860 saw work on two lighthouses advance: one at Race Rocks and the other on Fisgard Island, which improved maritime safety on a rocky lee shore.

Douglas continued to make arduous trips to meet Native bands on the mainland. It was a task he enjoyed and in which he was skilled. As he had done on Vancouver Island, he reassured them that land would be set aside for their needs, that they could hunt and fish as before, and that they could dig for gold like anyone else. Douglas also ensured that the Natives understood they were integral members of the new British colony.

Victoria, May 1861

Last year the shout of "Gold!" echoed again throughout the land west of the Rockies. Four miners discovered placer gold in Horsefly

Creek, a remote valley of the Cariboo region of British Columbia. Another strike in Williams Creek led to the mother lode. These finds were far, far richer than any around the Fraser and most required shafts to extract the gold. Although the miners tried to keep it secret, word inevitably spread, and now the two colonies are swamped by a second gold rush. Again, thousands of men are converging on us driven by greed and hope. Some Americans have come, but the U.S. Civil War and other finds in their own territory should restrict their numbers. Most prospectors hail from British North America.

I set off to verify the find. On my way north from Yale, I met prospectors heading to the coast with bulging sacks of gold. Two had enough to fetch $10,000, which had taken only five weeks to accumulate. Another had dug $525 worth in one day. These amounts of gold dust represent massive fortunes.

I will describe the implications of these finds to the British government with words like "incalculable wealth" and write of "future greatness" to encourage more investment in this colony they still view as minor.

Douglas established a Gold Escort — a heavily armed guard that took the gold to the assay office at Yale, leaving the miners to continue working their claims. But since Douglas couldn't guarantee safety, most miners chose to take their gold to Yale themselves. All carried rifles to protect their fortunes, but few thefts or fights occurred.

Of course, Douglas's second response, and an enduring one, was to build a road to Barkerville, a rough-and-ready shantytown deep in the Cariboo, north of Kamloops and south of Prince George. It was a colossal undertaking. Obstacles abounded, but Douglas's greatest problem was money, or rather the lack of it. The governor floated a loan for £50,000, the first in the history of British Columbia's government, but the project cost more than double that in the end.

The second obstacle was the mountains.

24

The Cariboo Wagon Road

James Douglas's bold plan, difficult to accomplish even today, was mind-boggling for its era. He ordered the construction of a wagon road 645 kilometres long and nearly six metres wide to start in the spring of 1862 for completion in early 1864. This was just the kind of project at which he excelled. His resolve was as rock-solid as the mountains the route had to penetrate; his single-mindedness was as focused as a prospector's eye spying a fleck of gold.

Victoria, November 1, 1861

The Cariboo Wagon Road is the next installment in my vision to link British territory from west to east. Once finished, I see this new road extending through the Rockies via the

Yellowhead Pass to Fort Edmonton, thence to Red River [now Winnipeg], using old brigade routes and following the north shore of Lake Superior until it finally arrives at Montreal. I couldn't contain a smile when I calculated that a road like this would allow travellers from Victoria to reach Red River in only twenty-five days. The fastest the *voyageurs* could manage was three to four months.

Although the Cariboo Wagon Road was Douglas's largest road project, it wasn't his first. That was the Douglas Trail built by miners in 1859, using Harrison Lake to reach Lillooet. Soon after that road opened, a crude thoroughfare linking Lillooet to Alexandria pushed northeastward through the inland plateau and was the reason that Lillooet became Mile 1 of the gold trail to the Cariboo, not Yale. Douglas's latest project incorporated and improved these two vital routes, named the Old Cariboo Road, at the beginning of the second gold rush. But since the roads couldn't accommodate wagons, supplies still had to travel on miners' backs or by mule train. It was a brutal journey to endure while the new road along the canyon was blasted through. Clinton, 100 Mile House, and Williams Lake got their start in this gold rush when roadhouses were built during the improvement phase to supply, feed, and house the miners during their arduous trek north.

Douglas contracted out much of the Cariboo Wagon Road construction to private organizations in the first private-public partnerships seen in British Columbia. He laced the offers to the companies with a strong incentive — he gave them the right to a share in the tolls on their sections of road for five to seven years to recoup their expenditures, while the colony poured its toll share into loan repayment. His decision to parcel out the work also allowed many sections to be constructed simultaneously.

The Royal Engineers tackled the most difficult sections in the Fraser Canyon from Yale to Lytton and along the Thompson River to Spence's Bridge. Parts of the road in the Fraser Canyon where the river cut through the Coastal Mountains required blasting rock away with explosives, while other sections needed trestle bridges to cross ravines. The main bridges at Spuzzum and Spence's Bridge to span the Fraser and the Thompson were built after the road was finished.

Yale, October 25, 1862

I am on a personal inspection tour of the roadworks. My report about Jackass Mountain, the Cleft, and the Great Slides will ignite considerable disbelief back in the England of rolling hills and sleepy villages. The Colonial Office in London has no conception of what we are doing here.

Settlers are already using the completed sections of the route and paying their tolls without a murmur, which gives my heart hope we will prevail on the financial side, too. The bridge tolls vary: large animals like oxen are charged a quarter per animal; a single-horse cart, a dollar; four-horse carts, two dollars. Local traffic passes free of charge, quite rightly.

At Spuzzum, where the brigades had lost so many horses and furs in 1848–49, a great suspension bridge was built in 1863

The Cariboo Wagon Road at Nicaragua Bluff in the Fraser Canyon showing the steep mountainsides, trestles, and guardrails.

to link the completed sections of roadway on either side. A remarkable feat of engineering in the mid-1800s, the structure was ninety-one metres long and robust enough to support heavily laden wagons safely. A bridge designed by Thomas Spence replaced the old rope ferry across the Thompson, changing the settlement's name from Cook's Ferry to Spence's Bridge. Douglas actually grinned as he proposed a toast in Victoria's mess hall to celebrate the completion of the major and most difficult sections of his project.

The bridges indeed marked a major turning point in the massive project by connecting the new road from Yale to the new section running north to Cache Creek and Clinton. At Clinton it joined the Old Cariboo Road. The Cariboo Wagon Road was now open for travellers from Yale to Alexandria. Work continued farther north from Alexandria to the mouth of the Quesnel River and widened the trail beyond that to the gold fields.

The opening of the road to Alexandria increased the toll revenue by 83 percent from the year before, which enabled Douglas to believe that the government share of toll revenues would eventually equal the expenditure. He sighed with relief. That left only the northerly section to finish and that was completed in the spring of 1864.

Victoria, September 15, 1863

I have just mailed a letter to London announcing our achievement. I can scarcely credit that today the journey from New Westminster to Alexandria takes only eight days. In fact, a fast stagecoach carrying only passengers can leave Yale and arrive in Barkerville in six and a half days. Progress!

I drew the Colonial Office a map to clarify how the journey from the coast to the Cariboo connects using a system of rivers and roads: a steamer to Hope, the Cariboo Wagon Road to Alexandria and Quesnel, and a horse trail to the gold fields.

I reminded London that farming had begun on the inland plateau and would immensely benefit from the road. I enclosed the dried and pressed wheat, oat, and barley ears I had picked to prove it. I estimate that by 1870 about a hundred thousand people will take advantage

of my Cariboo Wagon Road. How much gold it
will transport, I can't estimate exactly, but it will
be worth millions.[1]

At the end of 1863 Douglas was deeply satisfied with his
project. But after nearly six years of unrelenting pressure, he
needed a respite. He was feeling his years now, though he still
hadn't suffered a day of ill health.

25

Rewards and Retirement

In May 1863, James Douglas had learned, with mixed feelings, that the Colonial Office expected him to retire when his Vancouver Island governorship was up in September, a year before the end of his term in British Columbia. He wrote to London expressing that he was happy to relinquish Vancouver Island, but an early departure from the Colony of British Columbia might reflect poorly on him.

The colonial secretary politely suggested that his last official duty should be the opening ceremonies of the first Legislative Assembly of British Columbia at New Westminster in October 1863. Douglas, not willing to go quite so fast, requested a leave of absence to carry him through to the official ending of his governorship of British Columbia in September 1864. In the end, the Colonial Office extended his term on Vancouver Island to match that of the mainland and granted him leave from both in April 1864 until his retirement date in September. It was a win-win solution.

Queen Victoria awarded Douglas a knighthood in October 1863, recognizing his service to the British Empire. The illegitimate former fur trader from British Guiana became Sir James Douglas, K.C.B., and henceforth insisted that everyone address him as Sir James. He worked on through the turn of 1863 into February and March, writing letters and official dispatches that showed his zeal and attention to detail were as strong as ever.

With the newly appointed governor for Vancouver Island due to arrive in mid-March 1864, the glitterati of Victoria gave Sir James a retirement banquet a few days before to say farewell. Two hundred and fifty men attended the lavish affair at the Victoria Theatre, while fifty women observed the formal dinner from a discreet distance. Sir James listened to many glowing tributes, with ill feelings set aside for an evening, and accepted gifts that honoured his years of service. One that held special meaning for him was a small casket inlaid with Cariboo gold.

Since it wasn't customary for the outgoing governor to meet his replacement, Sir James and Lady Douglas left Victoria after the retirement celebrations. They sailed to New Westminster where he was to perform his last official duty for the Colony of British Columbia. Crowds joined the Douglases as they walked from their house to their ship in Victoria's harbour. A band joined the head of the procession and played "For He's a Jolly Good Fellow," and three cheers rang out as Sir James climbed the gangplank. When the SS *Otter* set sail, the band on board played "Auld Lang Syne" and the HBC staff fired a thirteen-gun salute. Sir James deeply appreciated his send-off.

His reception in New Westminster was in stark contrast. The mainland colonists didn't provide a rousing welcome. For

James Douglas in 1863.

a month the Douglases lived in Government House, which was being prepared for Frederick Seymour, the replacement everyone hoped would be better than Douglas. Sir James opened the Legislative Assembly on April 5 and listened to a farewell address in his honour that was understated but courteous. He attended another retirement banquet with about a hundred guests, but some of the invited refused to attend, including New Westminster's newspaper owner. The highlight of the evening for Sir James was the presentation of a testimonial to his service signed by more than nine hundred colonists. "Envy and malevolence may be endured," he said, "but your kindness overwhelms me."[1]

The last official act Sir James undertook in his long career was to grant the Stô:lo people of the Fraser Valley all the land they wished. He did so with great ceremony in New Westminster after he distributed gifts to all who came. His motivation, so late in his career, may have been to ensure one last grand gesture. Sadly, his expansive act never made it into law, and the Stô:lo lost their traditional territory.

After a less-than-happy month, Sir James and Lady Douglas departed New Westminster to avoid meeting Seymour and returned to Victoria where the new governor had already taken up his appointment. Their departure from British Columbia was even more subdued than their arrival — no crowds, no bands, and no cheering. Sir James only shrugged on hearing that the town had gone wild when Governor Seymour stepped onto the soil of New Westminster for the first time. Douglas was already onto his next project.

Sir James had only a month at home before he set off on an adventure of a lifetime. Now wealthy enough to travel in style, he was heading to Europe to enjoy a Grand Tour for twelve months. Sir James had taken neither a vacation nor a single sick day in more than forty-five years, and he had last seen Scotland when he was fifteen years old. Now he was overwhelmed with curiosity to see the world. Still energetic and in good health, he was as excited as a schoolboy. He busily planned how to connect with family he had never met; he wrote to friends telling them when to expect him; and he read guidebooks about the great cities of Europe that he couldn't wait to visit.

Douglas took his son, James, who was returning to school, and his trusted manservant, Edward, with him. Their journey to Britain took six weeks in a series of leaps across continents and oceans: first San Francisco, then to Panama and across the narrow isthmus into the Caribbean, across the Atlantic to the Azores, and finally to England.

Sir James spent the first three months exploring the length and breadth of Great Britain. He treated his thirteen-year-old son to all the sightseeing they could pack in before James Junior had to return to school in September. When his son went back to preparatory school, Sir James journeyed to Scotland by himself to meet his Glasgow relatives and enjoy his boyhood haunts. He also spent two weeks with his daughter, Jane, and her husband, Alexander Dallas, with whom he had fallen out. For the first time his composure collapsed. Sir James was overwhelmed with emotion at both his reunion with Jane and their farewell. And he restored his relationship with Dallas.

Choosing Paris as a base, Douglas travelled to most of the countries on the continent. He took an impressive eight-month tour and savoured every moment of it. Sir James noticed far more details than the average tourist and noted them all in his journal — sizes, quantities, prices, values, the unusual, and on and on. He eagerly sampled the food and wines of every region he visited. Sir James, at last, recognized how cut off he had been in Victoria and took every opportunity to discover the new politics and the ways administrations were managing their affairs in each nation he visited. New ideas and commentaries poured from his pen. He even included the effects of different faiths on various countries.

Douglas did everything a tourist should: he visited musty museums, the great art galleries, soaring cathedrals, fairy-tale castles, turquoise alpine lakes, and more. Pompeii and Herculaneum, which were the talk of Europe, riveted him. He adored Paris, which was a magnificent city, criss-crossed by wide boulevards and filled with beautiful architecture. Sir James's half-sister, whom he had never met, lived there, and Jane entertained him lavishly. Together they took in plays, ballets, operas, and concerts and attended soirees. His fluent French made everything all that more enjoyable.

Sir James shopped for himself and his family with abandon, spending a small fortune. After doing without the finer things of life for years, Douglas prowled the best stores and galleries in Europe, quenching his thirst for luxury and beauty. He didn't deny himself anything. His purchases sailed home on a Hudson's Bay Company supply ship, including more than 160 litres of good whisky, boxes and boxes of the latest fashions for his extended family, paintings, and for himself, a fine custom-made shotgun.

Over Christmas of 1865 and the New Year, Sir James caught up with his other two half-sisters, Cecilia and Georgina, who were holidaying at Pau, a delightful town in the French Pyrenees. They talked and talked, getting along famously. He discussed his son's education with them and concluded that it was time for James Junior to enter one of the big English public schools.

Unknown to her travelling husband, Lady Douglas was coping with yet another tragedy alone. Cecilia, their eldest daughter, now thirty, fell ill with pneumonia just before giving birth to a son. She survived the birth but died soon afterward. Her husband, John Helmcken, a doctor and the speaker of the Legislative Assembly, was unable to save her. Amelia took the death of her daughter harder than any of those before it. A friend stepped in to foster the baby, but sadly he died, too.

Sir James didn't hear about the loss of Cecilia until he returned to Paris. The news came in April, and he cut the rest of his plans short. His journal entries became briefer and more irregular from then on, indicating he had lost heart for both writing and travel. All he could think of was getting home. The grieving father returned to London, concluded some essential business, and took a passing look at the public school proposed for James. At the last minute he whisked his son out of school and took him home to ease his mother's bereavement.

26

Twilight

Father and son crossed the Atlantic Ocean in a very different mood from the anticipation in which they had sailed thirteen months before. They reached Victoria five full months after Cecilia died, the fastest Sir James could manage, and her death overshadowed this homecoming like so many in the past. Lady Douglas led her husband to their child's grave as she had done throughout their married life so he could grieve. And grieve he did.

However, gloom was hard to maintain in the Douglas household. Children filled their home with noise and laughter every day as ten-year-old Martha played with her Helmcken cousins from next door. Sir James grasped the right moments to tell his wife the details of his incredible trip and passed along the news of their daughter, Jane Dallas, and her family. When his purchases tumbled out of crates by the dozen, the family couldn't contain its delight.

Sir James noticed some changes to Victoria on arrival and was excited that the telegraph, which had reached New Westminster, would soon come to Vancouver Island. He learned with misgivings that the governor of Vancouver Island wasn't a good administrator and seemed incapable of handling an economic downturn. Sir James itched to fix the problems but didn't meddle. Instead, he turned to his own affairs and became more engaged in land development, mortgages, and investment. With pensions, rental income, and other revenues of nearly $30,000 a year and his family expenditure at $5,000, he was doing well and gave thanks for it. But like a typical Scot, he was apprehensive of "dying a beggar," according to Helmcken, his son-in-law.

Douglas had thrived on activity all his life and didn't change in retirement. He turned avidly to gardening and farming and became a gentleman farmer. Fairfield Farm captured most of his attention. Its 170 hectares grew crops and raised livestock, and Sir James supervised his tenant farmers himself. He began to develop a large tract called Rosedale he had bought west of Esquimalt's harbour, hoping the railway would end with a station on his land. He was disappointed — the defeat of Prime Minister Sir John A. Macdonald's Canadian government in 1873 terminated this money-making scheme.

Victoria, July 14, 1866

I ride out early every morning to do my rounds and return home for a hearty breakfast at 9:00 a.m. sharp. Often I take someone along for company — mostly my children, grandchildren, or nieces and nephews. I so enjoy having youngsters around me now that I have the time, and they seem to like coming with me. As my father did, I challenge them to try new things and teach them all I can about the world around them. My daughter, Martha, now twelve, is my most frequent companion, riding beside me on her white pony. I am enchanted by her intelligence and cheerful personality and hope to provide many opportunities for her. If Amelia joins me, we take our phaeton [a light two-horse carriage]. On other occasions I treat my friends, visitors, or business associates to my rounds. Deep snow doesn't prevent my daily excursions, either. I simply have the sleigh hitched up. Sometimes I spend all day overseeing my land and enjoying the countryside, as I did as a boy in Scotland. This activity rewards and relaxes me.

I also devote attention every day to reading books and writing letters, especially to my family and friends in Britain. If there is a good play or a concert, I attend them with Martha. Cards are still a favourite, too, and I play regularly at home.

One shadow remained that Sir James couldn't dispel. He had invested everything in his sole surviving son so that the boy could follow in his footsteps, but James Junior wasn't turning out the way he wished. After a summer in Victoria, Sir James sent his son back to boarding school in England with high hopes and lengthy advice on how to apply himself. Sir James hadn't yet grasped that fixing James Junior's frail health and lack of intellect was beyond his ability.

Alexander Dallas had persuaded Sir James that the well-known public school and demanding curriculum he had chosen for James Junior was likely to be a disaster. He suggested a smaller establishment in Hampshire with a more practical choice of subjects. Sir James reluctantly agreed and asked Dallas to keep an eye on the boy. Sadly, he remarked that at least this school might put some solid religion and backbone into his son.

However, Sir James stubbornly held on to the dream of his son going to Cambridge University and studying law. After the degree, he planned for James Junior to practise in London for a while before returning to Victoria as his pride and joy. He had long visualized James Junior entering the Legislative Assembly as an elected member. When his son failed to learn anything at the new school, he grew more desperate. Sir James kept moving his son to new schools in the vain expectation that he would improve. Incessantly, he fired off letters to his son that were critical and often insensitive. When read between the lines, they show how deeply embarrassed and frustrated Douglas was. His own intellect and good health prevented him from relating to his struggling, sickly heir.

When James Junior returned to Victoria after finishing school at nineteen, Sir James finally accepted how ill his son was. At last he abandoned the idea of the teenager attending university in England and took most of the pressure off by finding him work at a local law firm. James Junior did manage to win an election, thanks to his father's influence, and served as a member for Victoria in the Legislative Assembly from 1876 to 1878.

Sir James continued to follow the politics of the two colonies enthusiastically and felt betrayed when Vancouver Island and British Columbia were amalgamated in 1866 into the single Colony of British Columbia. He blamed not only the British government but also both assemblies for passing the resolutions

Image A-06864 courtesy Royal British Columbia Museum, B.C. Archives.

James William Douglas, the only son of James and Amelia, in 1880.

that brought the merger about, commenting it was a "sad, melancholy event."[1] He mourned the loss of Victoria's free-port status, but the real cause for his anguish, however, was that New Westminster would henceforth be the provincial capital. When the legislators changed their minds in 1868 and the capital returned to Victoria, he was unreservedly delighted.

British Columbia joined the Canadian Confederation in July 1871, relieving Britain of its distant colony. Sir James, who had been watching the process closely, didn't comment much even when the debate swirled through his family. He wasn't keen on the idea, but still fearing American expansionism, bowed to the inevitable. The majority of British Columbia residents viewed joining Canada with excitement. Victoria was now home to five thousand people. The shanties of the transient miners were gone, and brick buildings lined streets lit by gas lamps. Victorian propriety and respectability ruled.

As much as Sir James adored having Martha around, he also felt she needed the colonial roughness polished away and the training to become a sophisticated young woman. So he made the difficult decision to send her to finishing school for two years in England when she was eighteen. She left Victoria in August 1872. It was a sorrowful farewell for both parents. Lady Douglas collapsed with grief after the goodbyes. Sir James stifled his own emotion and comforted his wife as she cried herself into exhaustion.

Martha was all that James Junior could never be, and while she was in Europe, her father denied her nothing and pined for her company. They wrote long letters to each other during the separation. Despite the social whirl in London, Martha was homesick and begged to come home. But her father ignored the temptation and ordered her to complete her "improvement."

Sir James celebrated his sixty-ninth birthday two days after Martha sailed and was, by now, troubled with gout and occasional chest pains. With his favourite daughter gone, he withdrew from society. Boredom set in that he couldn't shake for the first time in his life, and as the end of the two-year separation from Martha approached, he became increasingly edgy.

James Douglas's beloved daughter, Martha, the year she went to finishing school in England, 1872.

Suddenly, the old fur trader packed up and left for London to bring Martha home, taking his trusty Edward with him. Instead of sailing directly to San Francisco, Sir James chose to travel by train through Washington State so he could relive some of his journeys around Fort Vancouver, then pick up a ship at the Columbia River mouth. At San Francisco he climbed stiffly into a first-class sleeper and rumbled across the continent to Chicago and New York. This was his first long train journey, and he marvelled at the speed and comfort. As he looked out the window, he recalled the many times he had trekked similar distances via canoe and snowshoe, as well as the forts where he had worked. It only took him twenty-eight days to reach his beloved Martha.

After a touching reunion, they travelled to Scotland and stayed with the Dallases at their country home in Invernessshire. There Sir James celebrated his seventy-second birthday in grand style, enjoying all the children and young people gathered about him. Jane noticed a decline in her father over the past decade: his eyes were sunken and his hair was pure white, and he was unsteady and had gained weight. Sir James, acutely aware he was close to the end of his life, took his son-in-law aside and asked him to act as executor of his will. When he and Martha left after a nine-day visit, the parting with Jane was painful. Sir James knew he would never see her again.

Douglas sailed with Martha via Liverpool to Montreal, a duplication of the voyage he had made as a teen in 1819, except he was in a steam-driven ship. He couldn't believe his eyes when he got to Montreal — what had been a small town so many years earlier was now a thriving city of 120,000. But he wasn't finished with nostalgia quite yet. He had one more sentimental journey to make before he went home.

In the morning Sir James put Martha on a steamer that stopped at Lachine later the same day. He needed to make this last trip alone. At Lachine he looked for the places he had seen as a fifteen-year-old, but most were gone. His father's words came back to him for the first time in years: "Work hard, behave properly, and obey your teachers!" As he walked slowly along the new canal, marvelling at the locks that provided shipping the means to reach the Great Lakes, he heard faint *chansons* of feisty *voyageurs* whispering around him. He observed the grey stone convent of the Sisters of Saint Anne from whose community Bishop Demers had plucked four nuns to open a school in Fort Victoria in 1858. Douglas remembered them vividly.

His mind roamed through the places and events he had experienced since setting off in his first canoe, and he considered how much he had done. He remembered the cruelly harsh winters, the fear of ambush, the lack of roads, his need for survival skills, and the many Natives he had admired. Sir James saw the faces of his friends and colleagues in the fur trade, many of whom were long dead. Now, he thought, Canada was filled with towns and villages, railways crossed the continent, and the telegraph provided almost instant communication. Slowly, he shook his head in wonder. Sir James took comfort in knowing the part he had played in opening up a country he had grown to love so much. He also realized how thankful he was not to be setting out by canoe for the west.

Once back home, Sir James led a less energetic life than before. On August 2, 1877, he took his customary carriage ride before breakfast, but late in the evening he became short of breath and complained of chest pains. His son-in-law, Dr. John Helmcken, hurried in from next door. While Sir James was chatting, his head suddenly fell back, and he was dead two weeks short of his seventy-fourth birthday. Sir James went quickly and peacefully, surrounded by his family.

Lady Douglas, who had been in poor health for years, surprised everyone by surviving her husband, a man who had followed an active routine to the end. In the midst of her grief she agreed to pleas for a state funeral. The body of Sir James lay in the family parlour as hundreds filed past the ornate rosewood casket to pay their last respects to the Father of British Columbia. The night before the funeral and unknown to anyone, Martha hid her father's precious David Thompson map beside him for his final journey.

Victoria spent four days of frenzied activity to prepare a fitting farewell. Businesses closed, flags flew at half-staff, and black fabric draped buildings in readiness for the biggest funeral Victoria had ever witnessed. On the appointed day, Marines and Royal Navy personnel formed an honour guard outside the Douglas home, while Edward Cridge, now a bishop of the Reformed Church, conducted a private service for the family and intimate friends in the parlour. Four grey horses drew the hearse across the harbour bridge behind the troops. On the far side the volunteer fire service and other civic groups met the cortege and led it to the Church of Our Lord. Mourners lined the streets united in silent grief and respect.

At the church the political elite and senior HBC officers carried Douglas's casket up the aisle, and a hundred Natives joined the procession. The church overflowed and the doors stood open for those outside to hear. Bishop Cridge performed the solemn service. All of Sir James's children attended except Jane and Alice. Even Bishop Hills took part out of his respect for Douglas, doing his best to hide his animosity toward Cridge who had opposed his leadership and broken with the Anglican

Church. As the hearse set out for Ross Bay Cemetery, the bells of the fire department and all the other churches began to toll. In the harbour HMS *Rocket* fired its guns at one-minute intervals. The procession of sixty-three carriages and a multitude on foot wound its way to the family plot.

The flag-draped casket passed through the ranks of sailors, Marines, and militia as it approached the vault, watched by a sombre crowd. Cridge presided over the last part of the day's ceremonies, and after the choir sang the final hymn, the honour guard fired three blank rounds and it was over. The Father of British Columbia was gone.

Several months after Sir James Douglas's funeral, his tombstone arrived from San Francisco. The massive monument of polished red granite with a Celtic cross on top dominated Ross Bay Cemetery just as Sir James had dominated in life.

Afterword

Sir James Douglas controlled his family in death as he had all his
life. His will of 1872 was complex. He had provided generous
trust funds for his wife and daughters and had donated to charities,
but most of his wealth went to his son: land, investments, farms,
possessions. James Junior, as Douglas's only male heir, inherited a
considerable fortune, but only benefited for a few years before his
own death passed it in trust to his young sons.

Martha, Sir James's favourite daughter, married Dennis
Harris the year after her father died. James Junior gave his sister
away at a high-society wedding performed by Bishop Cridge.
Then it was James's turn at the altar two months later when he
married May Elliott, the daughter of the province's premier. He
was a good catch from a financial viewpoint, but not otherwise
according to family and outsiders.

Lady Amelia Douglas was far from lonely in her bereavement

— her home was still bursting with family. James and Martha and their spouses, and daughter Agnes and her baby, lived with her, probably at her expense. Such close proximity meant disputes arose, and the strain lasted well into the 1880s. James and May soon left to rent a nearby house because of the discord. But though Martha and Dennis had built a home, they never moved into it, and Dennis became the acting head of the clan.

James and May went to Europe in 1883, seeking a cure in France for James's worsening Bright's disease (kidney failure). He didn't improve and died on November 7 in San Francisco on his way back to British Columbia. May brought his body to Victoria where it was laid to rest beside his father. Lady Douglas generously arranged for May to receive $3,000 per year from her own funds to support her daughter-in-law and the two boys until they were old enough to inherit their legacy.

Amelia spent her widowhood in seclusion, rarely leaving the family home. However, she made exceptions to host two glittering events, including her own seventy-fifth-birthday celebration and a garden party marking Queen Victoria's Golden Jubilee. Despite often talking about visiting her roots, she never undertook the long journey. When Amelia was seventy-seven, her health suddenly deteriorated. Within a month she was bedridden and cared for by Martha. In January 1890 she died, thirteen years after her husband. She had buried seven of her own children, but four daughters survived her and so did sixteen grandchildren and five great-grandchildren. Only Martha was with her mother at the end, but Agnes and Alice came from San Francisco for the funeral.

Lady Douglas's passing marked the beginning of the end of the Douglas family. James Junior's widow, May Douglas, and her two sons converted to Roman Catholicism in 1887, causing a major rift in the family. When May returned from

San Francisco after Lady Douglas's death to attend to business related to her boys' inheritance, she faced a family who, appalled that her Catholic sons would inherit Sir James's money, spitefully opposed her "popery." Martha's husband even took her to court to prevent James Junior's sons from attending Mass or Catholic schools in England. It was a mean-spirited action that failed, but it guaranteed that Douglas's grandsons would never return to the Pacific Northwest. Only Martha and her family stayed in Victoria, and the Douglas dynasty that Sir James had dreamed would flourish on Vancouver Island disappeared.

Despite his unpopularity in some quarters, his slow acceptance of democracy, and some misplaced favouritism, Douglas's vision and energy can't be questioned. He was a man of sharp intelligence and fierce drive that, coupled with unusual courage and a disciplined life, ensured success in the fur trade of the early 1800s. Later these traits overcame British apathy toward the far-flung Pacific frontier. While he was governor, Sir James took risks that resulted in many more positive outcomes than negative ones. He fought hard to secure British territory west of the Rocky Mountains for all time, instituted law and order during the gold rushes, and laid the foundation for land, water, and mineral rights. His passion for roads enabled infrastructure to open up and settle the region, and he maintained peace between First Nations and colonists while following a humanitarian philosophy in his dealings with blacks, aboriginals, and slaves.

When Sir James Douglas died, British Columbia was not only accelerating at the beginning of its drive toward prosperity but also heading in the right direction. The Father of British Columbia began that journey, carving a legacy bit by bit from a wild, formidable land because he believed with absolute conviction that his province was destined for greatness.

Notes

Chapter 4: Scotland and School

1. The Lanark Grammar School is still open today with a student body of a thousand.

Chapter 6: Postings and Promotions

1. The Cumberland House fort sat on an island in the Saskatchewan River delta on the edge of the Canadian Shield, about ninety kilometres from The Pas, Manitoba.
2. E.E. Rich, ed., *Journal of Occurrences*, cited in John Adams, *Old Square-Toes and His Lady* (Victoria, BC: Horsdal & Schubart, 2001), 16.

Chapter 7: Over the Shining Mountains

1. McLeod Lake is the oldest continuously inhabited European settlement in British Columbia, occupied from 1805 to the present day.

Chapter 8: *Un mariage à la façon du pays*

1. Chief Kwah's grave house still stands today where Stuart Lake empties into the Stuart River. The marker reads in English and Carrier: "Here lie the remains of Great Chief Kwah. Born about 1755. Died Spring of 1840. He once had in his hands the life of (future Sir) James Douglas but was great enough to refrain from taking it."

Chapter 10: Grief and Joy

1. Governor George Simpson's private "Book of Servants' Characters" held in the HBC archives, cited in Derek Pethick, *James Douglas: Servant of Two Empires* (Burnaby, BC: Mitchell Press, 1969), 27.

Chapter 11: Leadership

1. W.K. Lamb, "The James Douglas Report on the Beaver Affair," *Oregon Historical Quarterly*, 1946, cited in John Adams, *Old Square-Toes and His Lady* (Victoria, BC: Horsdal & Schubart, 2001), 48.

Chapter 12: Negotiator and Family Man

1. James Douglas, "April 1840–October 1841: Journal of Voyages to the North West Coast," 5. Library and Archives Canada, available online at *www.lac-bac.gc.ca/northern-star.*
2. E.S. Meany, ed., "Diary of Wilkes," *Washington Historical Quarterly*, XVI, no. 4 (October 1925), 299, cited in John Adams, *Old Square-Toes and His Lady* (Victoria, BC: Horsdal & Schubart, 2001), 56.

Chapter 13: Vancouver's Island

1. Douglas to James Hargrave, February 5, 1843, cited in John Adams, *Old Square-Toes and His Lady* (Victoria, BC: Horsdal & Schubart, 2001), 61.

Chapter 14: The End of Fort Vancouver

1. James Douglas to Sir George Simpson, March 19, 1849, cited in John Adams, *Old Square-Toes and His Lady* (Victoria, BC: Horsdal & Schubart, 2001), 71.

Chapter 15: Fort Victoria

1. The Royal British Columbia Museum now occupies the site.

Chapter 16: Governor at Last

1. Later called Beacon Hill Park, today it is a favourite with residents and visitors alike.

Chapter 18: Ruler, Not Politician

1. Today the islands between Vancouver Island and the continental mainland are called the Gulf Islands in Canadian waters and the San Juan Islands in U.S. waters.
2. The Crimean War (1853–56) pitted Britain, France, the Ottoman Empire, and the Kingdom of Sardinia against Russia and the Bulgarian Legion.

Chapter 19: Moving Toward Democracy

1. *Minutes of the House of Assembly of Vancouver Island: August 12, 1856, to September 25, 1858* (Victoria, BC: W.H. Cullin, 1918), Memoir No. III. Archives of British Columbia 20015319.

Chapter 20: The Fraser River Gold Rush

1. Mifflin W. Gibbs was one of the blacks who met with Douglas. He was a successful entrepreneur and was elected to Victoria's City Council in 1866. For the story of how this amazing man influenced the development of British Columbia, visit *http://thetyee.ca/Life/2008/02/07/MifflinGibbs*.

Chapter 21: Governor Again

1. Kinahan Cornwallis, *The New Eldorado; or British Columbia*, 1858 (2008 edition published by BiblioBazaar).
2. In fact, there was one very capable person, Alexander Dallas, a shareholder in the Hudson's Bay Company who was in Victoria on company business and had offered his services to James Douglas.

Chapter 24: The Cariboo Wagon Road

1. The Cariboo Wagon Road transported six and a half
   million dollars' worth of gold down to the coast between
   1864 and 1873.

Chapter 25: Rewards and Retirement

1. John Adams, *Old Square-Toes and His Lady* (Victoria, BC:
   Horsdal & Schubart, 2001), 158.

Chapter 26: Twilight

1. "Diary of Martha Douglas, 1866–69," entry by James Douglas,
   November 19, 1866. British Columbia Archives, cited in
   John Adams, *Old Square-Toes and His Lady* (Victoria, BC:
   Horsdal & Schubart, 2001), 175.

Chronology of
James Douglas
(1803-1877)

Compiled by Julie H. Ferguson

Douglas and His Times

Canada and the World

1670

A royal charter is granted by King Charles II of Britain to the Hudson's Bay Company (HBC) for exclusive trading rights in Rupert's Land, the drainage basin of Hudson Bay.

1770

David Thompson is born in London, England, to Welsh parents.

1774

The Hudson's Bay Company establishes its first inland fur-trading post at Cumberland

Douglas and His Times	*Canada and the World*
	House on the Saskatchewan River.

1783
The North West Company (NWC) is founded by a group of Montreal merchants to compete with HBC and expand the fur trade in British territory to the north and west.

1784
Russia founds a settlement in Alaska as well as a fur-trading post on Kodiak Island.

1790
Captain George Vancouver of Britain starts a three-year survey of the northwest coast of North America.

1791
The British divide Quebec into two colonies: Upper Canada (now Ontario) and Lower Canada (now Quebec).

Douglas and His Times	*Canada and the World*

1801

Alexander Douglas, James Douglas's older brother, is born to John Douglas and Martha Ann Ritchie in Demerara, British Guiana.

1803

James Douglas is born to John Douglas and Martha Ann Ritchie in Demerara, British Guiana.

1805

Simon Fraser establishes Fort McLeod in New Caledonia, the first NWC fort west of the Rocky Mountains.

1807

Britain abolishes the slave trade within its empire. The United States also abolishes the slave trade.

1808

NWC's Simon Fraser descends to the Pacific Ocean on the river that now bears

Douglas and His Times	*Canada and the World*

Canada and the World

his name. Fraser at first thinks he is travelling down the long-sought beginning of the Columbia River but eventually realizes he is mistaken.

John Jacob Astor sets up the American Fur Company.

1809
John Douglas marries Jessie Hamilton in Glasgow, Scotland.

1810
John Jacob Astor establishes the Pacific Fur Company, then sets sail on the *Tonquin* from New York City on a six-month voyage around South America to the Pacific West Coast where he founds a trading post at Astoria at the mouth of the Columbia River.

1812
Cecilia Douglas, James Douglas's sister, is born to John Douglas and Martha Ann Ritchie.

1812
The War of 1812 begins between Britain and the United States. The war is fought on Canadian and

Douglas and His Times

James Douglas sails to
Scotland with his father and
Alexander to go to school.

1819
Douglas sails onboard the
brig *Matthews* for Montreal
to become a fur trader with
the North West Company and
winters in Fort William (now
Thunder Bay, Ontario).

Canada and the World

American territory and ends
in 1814, though the last battle
is fought in January 1815.

1814
David Thompson finishes a
large map of the Northwest
from Lake Superior to the
Pacific Ocean. This map
hangs for many years in the
Great Hall of NWC's interior
headquarters at Fort William
on Lake Superior.

1816
The Seven Oaks Massacre
takes place in the Red River
Colony, and Lord Selkirk
invades Fort William.

Douglas and His Times	*Canada and the World*

1820–25
Douglas is an apprentice clerk at Fort Île-à-la-Crosse.

1821
When the North West Company merges with the Hudson's Bay Company, Douglas becomes an HBC man.

1821
The Hudson's Bay Company and the North West Company merge under the former's name. George Simpson becomes governor of the new Northern Department of HBC.

1824
Dr. John McLoughlin is appointed chief factor of the Columbia Department.

The Lachine Canal bypassing the rapids at Montreal is finished.

1825
Douglas is a temporary clerk at Fort Vermilion, then becomes the senior clerk at Fort St. James, New Caledonia.

1826
George Simpson is appointed

Douglas and His Times	*Canada and the World*
	governor of both the Northern and Southern Departments of HBC.
1828 Douglas marries Amelia Connolly, the daughter of William Connolly, the chief factor of New Caledonia.	
1830 Douglas is appointed accountant at Fort Vancouver.	
	1833 Britain abolishes slavery in its empire, including its colonies in North America.
1835 Douglas becomes chief trader at Fort Vancouver.	
	1836 SS *Beaver* begins service for HBC on the Pacific coast.
	1837 Queen Victoria ascends the

Douglas and His Times	**Canada and the World**
	throne in Britain.
1838 Douglas is appointed acting chief factor of the Columbia Department.	**1837–38** Rebellions break out in Upper and Lower Canada but are quickly suppressed by the British and their colonial representatives. The rebels, led by William Lyon Mackenzie in Upper Canada and Louis-Joseph Papineau in Lower Canada, want their respective colonies to have more say in their own affairs.
1839 Martha Ann, Douglas's mother, dies in British Guiana.	**1839** George Simpson is appointed governor of Rupert's Land.
1840 Douglas is appointed chief factor of Columbia Department. John Douglas, James's father, dies.	
1841 Douglas first visits Vancouver Island.	**1841** Upper Canada becomes Canada West and Lower

Douglas and His Times	*Canada and the World*
	Canada becomes Canada East in a new United Province of Canada.
1842 Douglas chooses the site for Fort Victoria.	
	1843 HBC builds Fort Victoria on the southern tip of Vancouver Island to strengthen the British claim to the area and to guarantee access to the mainland via the Fraser River.
	1846 The Oregon Treaty settles the boundary between British and U.S. territory at the forty-ninth parallel.
1849 Douglas and his family move permanently to Fort Victoria.	**1849** Fort Victoria becomes the HBC headquarters of the Columbia Department. The Colony of Vancouver Island is established, with

Douglas and His Times	Canada and the World
	Richard Blanshard as its first governor.
	The California gold rush begins.
1851 Douglas is appointed governor of the Colony of Vancouver Island.	
1853 Douglas is appointed lieutenant governor of the Queen Charlotte Islands.	
	1854 Britain, France, the Ottoman Empire, and the Kingdom of Sardinia begin the Crimean War against Russia.
	1857 David Thompson dies in Longueuil, Canada East.
	Bytown, renamed Ottawa, is chosen as the capital of the United Province of Canada.

Douglas and His Times

Canada and the World

John McLoughlin, former
HBC patron of Douglas, dies.

1858
Douglas is commissioned
as governor of the Colony
of British Columbia at Fort
Langley.

1858
The Fraser River gold rush
begins.

The Colony of British
Columbia is established.

1860
George Simpson dies.

1863
Queen Victoria rewards
Douglas with a knighthood.

1860–63
Construction of the Cariboo
Wagon Road takes place.

1864
Douglas retires and visits
Europe for the first time since
1819.

1861–65
U.S. Civil War is fought
between the Union North and
the Confederate South.

1866
The Colonies of Vancouver
Island and British Columbia
merge.

1867
The United Province of

Douglas and His Times	*Canada and the World*

Canada and the World

Canada (Canada West and East), Nova Scotia, and New Brunswick join together in Confederation to become the Dominion of Canada. Canada West becomes Ontario; Canada East becomes Quebec.

The United States purchases Russian Alaska and sandwiches British Columbia between two American territories.

1868
HBC gives up its trading monopoly and transfers title of Rupert's Land to Canada in exchange for £300,000, the lands around its trading posts, and one-twentieth of the agricultural lands on the Prairies.

1869–70
The Red River Rebellion, led by Louis Riel, breaks out in what is now Manitoba. The rebels demand and receive

Douglas and His Times	*Canada and the World*
	provincial status in Canada for Manitoba in 1870. Riel goes into exile.
	1871 British Columbia joins Confederation as the sixth Canadian province.
	1873 Prince Edward Island joins Confederation, bringing the total Canadian provinces to seven.
1874 Douglas returns to Britain to bring his daughter, Martha, home.	
1877 Sir James Douglas dies.	
1883 James Douglas, Jr., dies.	
	1885 The North-West Rebellion, an uprising of Métis and Cree

Douglas and His Times	*Canada and the World*

Canada and the World

led by Louis Riel and Cree chiefs such as Poundmaker and Big Bear in the District of Saskatchewan, breaks out but is swiftly put down by Canadian militia and the newly formed North-West Mounted Police. Soon after, Louis Riel is hanged for high treason.

The last spike of the Canadian Pacific transcontinental railway is driven home.

1886
Vancouver is incorporated as a city.

First passenger train arrives at Port Moody, British Columbia, from eastern Canada.

1890
Lady Amelia Douglas dies.

Sources Consulted

Many more sources are available. I have chosen to list more recently published books.

Books

Adams, John. *Old Square-Toes and His Lady.* Victoria, BC: Horsdal & Schubart, 2001.

Bagshaw, Roberta, ed. *No Better Land: The 1860 Diaries of the Anglican Colonial Bishop George Hills.* Victoria, BC: Sono Nis Press, 1996.

Campbell, Marjorie W. *The Nor'Westers: The Fight for the Fur Trade.* Toronto: Macmillan of Canada, 1954.

Ferguson, Julie H. *Sing a New Song: Portraits of Canada's Crusading Bishops.* Toronto: Dundurn Press, 2006.

Hauka, Donald J. *McGowan's War.* Vancouver: New Star Books, 2003.

Hume, Stephen. *Simon Fraser: In Search of Modern British Columbia.* Madeira Park, BC: Harbour Publishing, 2008.

Johnston, Hugh J.M., ed. *The Pacific Province: A History of British Columbia.* Vancouver: Douglas & McIntyre, 1996.

Langston, Laura. *Pay Dirt! The Search for Gold in British Columbia.* Victoria, BC: Orca, 1995.

Lunn, Janet, and Christopher Moore. *The Story of Canada.* Toronto: Key Porter Books and Lester Publishing, 1992.

Molyneux, Geoffrey. *British Columbia: An Illustrated History.* Vancouver: Polestar, 1992.

Newman, Peter C. *Company of Adventurers.* Toronto: Penguin Canada, 2004.

Ormsby, Margaret A. *British Columbia: A History.* Toronto: Macmillan of Canada, 1958.

Perry, Kenneth E. *Frontier Forts and Posts of the Hudson's Bay Company.* Surrey, BC: Hancock House, 2006.

Pethick, Derek. *James Douglas: Servant of Two Empires.* Vancouver: Mitchell Press, 1969.

Pritchard, Allan, ed. *Vancouver Island Letters of Edmund Hope Verney 1862–65.* Vancouver: University of British Columbia Press, 1996.

Sterne, Netta. *Fraser Gold 1958!* Pullman, WA: Washington State University Press, 1998.

Papers

Girard, Charlotte S.M. "Sir James Douglas's School Days." *BC Studies* No. 35 (Autumn 1977): 56–63.

____. "Sir James Douglas's Mother and Grandmother." *BC Studies* No. 44 (Winter 1979–80): 25–31.

____. "Some Further Notes on the Douglas Family." *BC Studies* No. 72 (Winter 1986–87): 3–27.

Hauka, Donald J. "Ned McGowan's War." *The Beaver: Exploring Canada's History* (February 2003).

Killian, Crawford. "B.C.'s Amazing Black Pioneer: Why Mifflin Gibbs Still Matters Today." *The Tyee* (February 7, 2008): *thetyee.ca/Life/2008/02/07/MifflinGibbs*.

____. "B.C.'s Black Pioneers Arrived 150 Years Ago Today: Why They Came." *The Tyee* (April 25, 2008): *www.thetyee.ca*.

Mackie, Richard. "The Colonization of Vancouver Island." *BC Studies* No. 96 (Winter 1992–93): 3–40.

Acknowledgements

Writing a book like this one takes many individuals in addition to the author. My first choice for the foreword of this biography was Stephen Hume, a journalist and author I have long admired but never met. I could scarcely contain my delight when he replied to my request in less than an hour. Not only that, he agreed to write the foreword. I am deeply grateful for his generosity, and for his words, which open this book.

As always, I must thank my Port Moody writers' group for its enduring support, motivation, and constructive criticism given so liberally over twenty years: Eileen Kernaghan, novelist, for her wise leadership; Joyce Gram, colleague and editor, for her clarity; Addena Sumter-Freitag for her astute insights into the black mind; Doug Matthews for his gift of boyhood books on the fur trade; and all the other members who chimed in with helpful suggestions for this book.

I must thank my editor, Michael Carroll, at Dundurn Press for the idea and having confidence that I could indeed write a book in four months when I scarcely believed it myself. My appreciation also goes to the rest of the Dundurn staff who had a hand in getting *James Douglas* published. For all our sakes, I hope it has long legs.

Lastly, I thank all who read and enjoy this book. I hope the beginnings of our wild and beautiful province have captivated you as much as it did me.

Index

Numbers in *italics* refer to images.